Sounds Real!

Authentic Listening and Speaking Practice

Allyson MacKenzie   Hidemori Yasuyama

TSURUMI SHOTEN

SOUNDS REAL!
Authentic Listening and Speaking Practice

Copyright© 2015 by Allyson MacKenzie, Hidemori Yasuyama
and OTOWASHOBO TSURUMISHOTEN

All rights reserved.

No part of this book may be used or reproduced
without the written permission of the publisher.

Photo Credits:

© petunyia—Fotolia.com
© Jeanette Dietl—Fotolia.com
© Olesia Bilkei—Fotolia.com
© Sasa Komlen—Fotolia.com
© elitravo—Fotolia.com
© 3dmentat—Fotolia.com
© Rawpixel—Fotolia.com
© evgenyb—Fotolia.com
© atomos19—Fotolia.com
© Halfpoint—Fotolia.com
© paylessimages—Fotolia.com
© Monkey Business—Fotolia.com
© Africa Studio—Fotolia.com
© pressmaster—Fotolia.com
© TOMO—Fotolia.com

INTRODUCTION

Toshi is a Japanese university student who is getting ready to study abroad. In the first two chapters he is preparing for his trip. The next twelve chapters follow him on his journey at an American university. First he has to get ready for the start of the school year. Then, he makes friends, learns about culture and customs from them and he even applies for a part-time job at his exchange university.

The book is set up into 14 main chapters with a final review chapter. The focus of the book is on listening and speaking using natural English, and the aim is to help you to feel more confident using and listening to English with natural, relaxed pronunciation.

Each chapter begins with **VOCABULARY PREVIEW**. You will practice some of the more challenging words and expressions from the chapter. You have to negotiate the spelling and meaning of each word with your classmates.

Useful Phrases boxes (see below) appear throughout the chapters to help you to have more confidence to ask your classmates for their ideas and opinions and for you to give yours. Preview the phrases and use them to get the most benefit out of your English class time!

Useful phrases　この表現を使って話し合ってみよう

What did you hear for number ~ ?　　How do you spell ~ ?
I heard ~　　　　　　　　　　　　　　I think it's spelled _ _ _ _ _

The **SHORT DIALOG** focuses on natural conversation and pronunciation. Try to notice and use relaxed English pronunciation. This will help you to get better at understanding English as it is spoken.

In the **PRONUNCIATION** section you'll practice using expressions from the dialog. This will help your pronunciation to become more natural and people will understand you better.

The **SPEAKING** section gives you the chance to communicate using useful patterns and also to review some of the points presented in the chapters. You will get more information or review a theme from the chapter, or you'll practice some of the points you heard in the dialog or the pronunciation section.

Finally, the **PROVERBS AND SAYINGS** section presents you with an interesting or humorous saying connected to the theme of the chapter. This will help you to become familiar with some popular sayings from a variety of famous people through the ages.

The book ends with a final review chapter. How much of what you studied will you remember? It goes without saying that the more you use the useful phrases and speak in English in class the more you will learn and remember. Do your best to speak in English, and good luck!

はじめに

本テキストは、ナチュラルな英語のリスニングとスピーキングの練習に主眼を置いており、自然でなめらかにつながった発音の英語を聴きとったり、実際に使ったり出来るようになることを目標としています。

本書は全15章から成ります。テキストの主人公である日本人学生 Toshi は、California の大学に留学します。冒頭の2章では彼の渡航の準備の様子を、それにつづく各章ではアメリカでの大学生活のさまざまな場面を扱っています。Toshi は、入学手続きに始まり、友人との交流、異なる文化や習慣の体験、あるいは大学でのパートタイムの仕事への応募など、いろいろな経験をしていきます。

本書の特徴として、全章を通して、***Useful Phrases*** という下のような囲みが登場します。クラスメートと「英語で」意見やアイデアを交換する時に活用します。授業以外でも英会話のきっかけ作りのためにぜひ活用してみてください。

Useful phrases　この表現を使って話し合ってみよう

What did you hear for number ~ ?　　　　How do you spell ~ ?
I heard ~　　　　　　　　　　　　　　　I think it's spelled _ _ _ _ _

各章は、まず **VOCABULARY PREVIEW** から始まります。ここでは重要な単語や表現を練習します。つづりや意味をクラスメートと「英語で」話し合って答えを確認します。

SHORT DIALOG では会話を聴いていくつかの質問に答えます。ここでは、自然な発音と会話表現の習得に主眼を置いていますので、なめらかにつながった発音を意識し、実際に使ってみましょう。英語の話し言葉に、より親しむことが出来るようになるでしょう。

PRONUNCIATION では、Short Dialog で使われていた表現を使って発音の練習をします。自然な発音を身につけ、より通じる英語を話すことに役立てましょう。

SPEAKING にはさまざまな activity が用意されており、Dialog や Pronunciation で学んだ各章の重要な学習事項を再確認し強化することができます。

PROVERBS AND SAYINGS では、各章のテーマと関連したことわざや名言を扱います。古今のさまざまな教訓に親しむことが出来るでしょう。

テキストの最後の章は全体の復習です。本書で学習したことはどれくらい身についているでしょうか。授業の中で Useful Phrases を活用するなどしてたくさん英語を話すことを心がけたあなたは、きっと英語力が向上していますよ。Good luck!

［音声トラック番号の表記について］

　　　　CD 1-2　= CD 1枚目のトラック2
　　　　DL 2　　= ダウンロード用音声のトラック2

TABLE OF CONTENTS

Chapter 1	**TOSHI'S BIG DAY** (Travel 1)	1
Chapter 2	**THE ADVENTURE BEGINS!** (Travel 2)	7
Chapter 3	**ORIENTATION DAY** (University 1)	13
Chapter 4	**CAREER ADVICE** (University 2)	19
Chapter 5	**A WELCOME PARTY** (Friends 1)	25
Chapter 6	**BREAK A LEG!** (Friends 2)	31
Chapter 7	**A SPECIAL INVITATION** (Family 1)	37
Chapter 8	**A WEDDING RECEPTION** (Family 2)	43
Chapter 9	**A TEXT MESSAGE** (Relationships 1)	49
Chapter 10	**A BLIND DATE** (Relationships 2)	55
Chapter 11	**APPLYING FOR WORK** (Work 1)	61
Chapter 12	**A JOB INTERVIEW** (Work 2)	67
Chapter 13	**SPANISH LESSONS** (Future plans 1)	73
Chapter 14	**SPRING BREAK** (Future plans 2)	79
Chapter 15	**REVIEW**	85

Chapter 1 TOSHI'S BIG DAY
(Travel 1)

VOCABULARY PREVIEW

1 Pronunciation Practice [CD 1-2/DL 2]
英語の単語や表現を聞いて口頭で繰り返してください。

2 Dictation [CD 1-2/DL 2]
もう一度同じ単語や表現を聞き下の1~8番の空欄に記入しましょう。次にスペルが正しく書けているかどうか隣同士ペアになってチェックし合います。その際、下の囲み内の表現を使いながら英語で相談してみましょう。

> *Useful phrases*　この表現を使って話し合ってみよう
> What did you hear for number ~ ?　　How do you spell ~ ?
> I heard ~　　　　　　　　　　　　　I think it's spelled _ _ _ _ _

1. __abroad_____ (h)　　5. _____ (   )
2. _____ (   )　　6. _____ (   )
3. _____ (   )　　7. _____ (   )
4. _____ (   )　　8. _____ (   )

3 Definitions
3、4人のグループを作ります。上の8つの単語や表現の定義として最もふさわしいものを下から選び、上のカッコ内に記号を記入しましょう。辞書は使わずにグループ内で英語で話し合って答えを選びます。その際、下の囲み内の表現を使ってみましょう。

a. to put something in a bag or suitcase to take with you
b. arranged or planned in a neat or effective way
c. a brother of your husband / wife, or your sister's husband
d. to have a reason for doing something
e. showing feelings of being worried of what might happen
f. happening or occurring soon
g. an important day
h. in or to a foreign country

> *Useful phrases*　この表現を使って話し合ってみよう
> Are you ready? I'll read the definition and you choose the best word.
> What is ~ ?　　　　　　　　　　I'm not sure. Maybe it is ~
> I think so too.　　　　OR　　　I agree.
> I disagree. I think the answer is ~ .

SHORT DIALOG

まず右の頁の質問文に目を通してから会話文 (Part 1) を読みましょう。次に会話を聴いてそれぞれの質問に答えます。会話文の後半 (Part 2) は印刷されていませんので集中して聴きましょう。

> ***Situation***: Toshi is at his university's International Exchange Center. He is speaking with Mr. Price, the International Exchange Student Adviser.

Part 1

[1] [CD 1–3/DL 3]

Mr. Price: Hey Toshi, I guess the big day is coming up. How are you feeling?

Toshi: Hi Mr. Price. I'm starting to get excited and I also feel **sort of** nervous. There is still so much I **have to** do. My flight leaves in one week.

Mr. Price: Good, you have your ticket and your student visa. Have you started to pack yet?

[2] [CD 1–4/DL 4]

Toshi: I bought my airplane ticket last month and I have my student visa, too. I guess I **have to** start to think about what I should bring with me.

Mr. Price: You should make a list of the things you want to pack. That will help you to be more organized.

Toshi: That's really good advice. I **ought to** start making my list today.

[3] [CD 1–5/DL 5]

Mr. Price: Is this your first time to travel abroad Toshi?

Toshi: No, my family took a weeklong trip to Hawaii when I was in elementary school and I spent a month in California visiting my older sister last year. Her husband works for a Japanese company in Los Angeles.

Mr. Price: Really? I didn't know that.

The conversation continues in Part 2.

Notes

student visa「学生ビザ」ビザ（査証）—海外渡航をする人々に対して、入国側の政府が審査を経て与える入国許可（証）のこと。渡航目的によって種類の異なるビザが発行されるが、主なものとして、tourist visa「観光ビザ」、student visa「学生ビザ」、working visa「就労ビザ」などがある。なお、student visa「学生ビザ」の場合は通常、留学を予定している大学や専門学校からの入学許可を受けて、滞在予定国の大使館から発行される。

Question 1: What will Toshi do next week?
  A. He'll sort out his flight.
  B. He'll go abroad.
  C. He'll buy a ticket.

Question 2: What advice does Mr. Price give to Toshi?
  A. Make a list.
  B. Be more organized.
  C. Buy a ticket.

Question 3: How much time has Toshi already spent abroad?
  A. One week.
  B. Four weeks.
  C. Five weeks.

Part 2 [CD 1-6~8/DL 6~8]

Question 4: Toshi's brother-in-law is not good at English.
  T   F

Question 5: Toshi says he wants to work abroad.
  T   F

Question 6: Toshi will plan what he needs for his trip.
  T   F

Notes
  weeklong「一週間の」/ **at the moment**「今のところ、目下のところ」/ **improve**「向上させる、伸ばす」
  / **to tell you the truth**「本当のことを言うと、実を言うと」/ **motivated**「やる気のある」

PRONUNCIATION　ポイント：①音の連結と脱落　②弱母音の発音 [ə]

自然な速さで英文を発音すると、単語同士の間隔が狭まり、音がつながることが起こります。ときにはまったく新しい音が生まれることもあります。

ルール：下のような語句を自然な速さで発音するとき、音同士のつながりが起こり、完全に脱落する音や新たに生まれる音があります。それぞれの最後の音（母音）はうめくような弱い「ア」で、弱母音と呼ばれるものです。

1 Practice 1　[CD 1-9/DL 9]

音声の後に続けて発音してみましょう。

Sort of	= Sorta
Kind of	= Kinda
Have to	= Hafta
Ought to	= Oughta

註：「ought to」は相手に助言を与える時の表現です。助言を聞き入れれないと、悪いことや好ましくないことが起こる含意があります。

2 Practice 2　[CD 1-10/DL 10]

音声を聞いて、下の例文を練習しましょう。まず、通常の発音での文が流れます。次に、音同士がつながった形の文が流れます。ペアの相手と両方の形の例文を発音してみましょう。

I **ought to** start making my list.	I *oughta* start making my list.
I feel **sort of** nervous.	I feel *sorta* nervous.
There is so much I **have to** do.	There is so much I *hafta* do.

3 Practice 3　[CD 1-11/DL 11]

下の文を読み、上の例文の太字の語句の中から適切なものを選び、空欄を埋めましょう。音声を聞いて答えをチェックしてみましょう。

Example: The color of the ocean is <u>sort of</u> bluish green.

1. I want to lose 10 kg so I _____ exercise more and eat less.
2. You really _____ bring an umbrella with you. It looks like rain.
3. The quiz was _____ difficult so I'm not sure if I passed it.

上で学習した発音を特に意識して、2 頁の会話をペアの相手と練習してみましょう。

SPEAKING [Talking about the time and routines]

1 Practice 1

あなたの一日は何時に始まりますか？ 例にならって１から13の空欄に時間を記入して自分の典型的な一日の行動を完成させましょう。14から16の空欄にはこれ以外にあなたが日常的にすることと、その時間を書き入れなさい。すべておおよその時間で構いません。

Daily routine / Time　　　**Daily routine / Time**

Example:　I wake up at 6:30 a.m.　　I take a shower at 7:00 a.m.

Your daily routine　　/　　Time

1. I wake up at _____ .
2. I take a shower at _____ .
3. I get dressed at _____ .
4. I eat breakfast at _____ .
5. I brush my teeth at _____ .
6. I go to university at _____ .
7. I eat lunch at _____ .
8. I talk with friends at _____ .
9. I eat dinner at _____ .
10. I do homework at _____ .
11. I work part-time at _____ .
12. I take a bath at _____ .
13. I go to bed at _____ .
14. I _____ at _____ .
15. I _____ at _____ .
16. I _____ at _____ .

完成したら、ペアになってお互いの一日の行動について質問し合います。相手の質問を注意して聴いて答えましょう。14から16に書いたあなたの行動は相手もするでしょうか。ぜひ聞いてみましょう。

Useful phrases　　この表現を使って話し合ってみよう

What time do you ___wake up___ ?　　I _____ at ____:____

Chapter 1　TOSHI'S BIG DAY (Travel 1)　5

PROVERBS AND SAYINGS

1 Practice 1 [CD 1-12/DL 12]

英語のことわざ（名言）を（必要に応じて）数回聴いて書き取ります。次にグループになって書き取ったものを比べてみます。もう一度音声を聴いて、必要があれば訂正しながらグループの答えを書きましょう。最終的に全員が正答にたどり着けるようにしましょう。

1. _____ (9 words)

2 Practice 2

グループ内でこのことわざ（名言）の意味について話し合ってa～cの中から正解を選びましょう。

a. When visiting foreign countries I stay in expensive hotels.
b. I like to visit foreign countries more than to stay at home.
c. When visiting foreign countries I enjoy feeling uncomfortable.

Useful phrases　この表現を使って話し合ってみよう

What did you hear?	What did you write?
What word did you write before ____?	What word did you write after ____?
How do you spell _____?	Look at my answer. Is anything missing?
What does ___ mean in Japanese?	What does this saying mean?

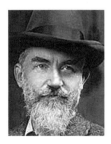

Chapter 2 THE ADVENTURE BEGINS! (Travel 2)

VOCABULARY PREVIEW

1 Pronunciation Practice [CD 1-13/DL 13]
英語の単語や表現を聞いて口頭で繰り返してください。

2 Dictation [CD 1-13/DL 13]
もう一度同じ単語や表現を聞き下の1～8番の空欄に記入しましょう。次にスペルが正しく書けているかどうか隣同士ペアになってチェックし合います。その際、下の囲み内の表現を使いながら英語で相談してみましょう。

Useful phrases この表現を使って話し合ってみよう
What did you hear for number ~ ? 　　How do you spell ~ ?
I heard ~ 　　　　　　　　　　　　　　I think it's spelled _ _ _ _ _

1. _aisle_____ (c)   5. _____ (   )
2. _____ (   )   6. _____ (   )
3. _____ (   )   7. _____ (   )
4. _____ (   )   8. _____ (   )

3 Definitions
3、4人のグループを作ります。上の8つの単語や表現の定義として最もふさわしいものを下から選び、上のカッコ内に記号を記入しましょう。辞書は使わずにグループ内で英語で話し合って答えを選びます。その際、下の囲み内の表現を使ってみましょう。

a. the place at an airport where government officers check your passport and things you have with you
b. an expression used when you look at something carefully to make sure nothing is wrong
c. a passage space between seats in a theater, airplane, etc.
d. a period of time when you stop at a place on a journey
e. a special machine used to check the weight of something
f. a special paper that lists the places you will be going to
g. a special piece of paper you need to get onto an airplane
h. equipment or a machine made for a special purpose

Useful phrases この表現を使って話し合ってみよう
Are you ready? I'll read the definition and you choose the best word.
What is ~ ?　　　　　　　　　　　I'm not sure. Maybe it is ~
I think so too.　　　　　OR　　　　I agree.
I disagree. I think the answer is ~ .

SHORT DIALOG

まず右の頁の質問文に目を通してから会話文 (Part 1) を読みましょう。次に会話を聴いてそれぞれの質問に答えます。会話文の後半 (Part 2) は印刷されていませんので集中して聴きましょう。

Situation: Toshi is at the airport checking in and preparing to get on to his flight.

Part 1

[1] [CD 1–14/DL 14]

Agent: Good afternoon sir. Where are you flying to today?
Toshi: **I am** flying to Los Angeles with a stopover in San Francisco.
Agent: May I see your passport and a copy of your flight itinerary please?

[2] [CD 1–15/DL 15]

Toshi: Here you are.
Agent: Please place the baggage that **you will** be checking in today up on the scale. Would you prefer a window or an aisle seat?
Toshi: I have these two suitcases and a small carry-on bag. **I would** like an aisle seat please. Also, I have a stopover in San Francisco. Will I have to check my baggage there again?

[3] [CD 1–16/DL 16]

Agent: Yes, **you will** have to collect your baggage in San Francisco and go through customs and immigration there. Then **you will** need to re-check your luggage for your flight to Los Angeles.
Toshi: Okay, I understand. Thank you.
Agent: Here are your boarding passes. Your seat number is 32D. Your flight leaves from gate 14 at 2:30 pm. **It will** begin boarding at 2:00 pm so please make sure to be at the gate before boarding begins.

The conversation continues in Part 2.

Notes

stopover「乗り継ぎ、途中降機」正式には乗り継ぎ地点で 24 時間以上滞在するものを stop-over と呼ぶ。／**itinerary**「旅行日程」／**carry-on**「機内持ち込みの」／**destination**「目的地、行き先」／**collect**「受け取る、集める」／**go through**「通過する、通り抜ける」／**customs**「税関」／**immigration**「入国審査」

Question 1: What does the airline agent ask Toshi to give to her?

  A. Both his passport and suitcase
  B. Both his passport and flight details
  C. Only his itinerary

Question 2: Does Toshi have a direct flight to his final destination?

  A. Yes, it goes from Narita to Los Angeles.
  B. Yes, it goes from Narita to San Francisco.
  C. No, his first flight stops in San Francisco.

Question 3: What does Toshi need to do in San Francisco?

  A. He needs to collect his baggage.
  B. He needs to study American customs.
  C. He needs to be there before 2:00 p.m.

Part 2 [CD 1-17~19/DL 17~19]

Question 4: Security must check Toshi's carry-on items before he may board the airplane.

  T   F

(Toshi is going through security check.)

Question 5: Toshi must take his computer out of its case.

  T   F

(Toshi is going through immigration)

Question 6: Toshi checks inside his bag for his boarding pass.

  T   F

Notes

departure「出発」／ **passport control**「出入国審査」immigration と passport control は同義語として扱われているが、immigration は主に入国審査を意味するために使われる。／ **remove**「外す、取り除く」

PRONUNCIATION   ポイント：短縮形の発音時の母音の脱落

自然な速さで文を発音すると、単語同士の間隔が狭まった結果、音がつながる現象が起こります。ときには完全に消滅してしまう音もあります。

ルール：下のような語句を自然な速さで発音するとき、音同士の自然なつながりが起こり、母音が完全に脱落します。

1 Practice 1 [CD 1-20/DL 20]

音声の後に続けて発音してみましょう。

I am	= I'm
I will	= I'll
I would	= I'd
You will	= You'll
It will	= It'll

2 Practice 2 [CD 1-21/DL 21]

音声を聞いて、下の例文を練習しましょう。まず、通常の発音での文が流れます。次に、音同士がつながった形の文が流れます。ペアの相手と両方の形の例文を発音してみましょう。

I am flying to Los Angeles.   *I'm* flying to Los Angeles.
I would like an aisle seat please.   *I'd* like an aisle seat please.
It will begin boarding at 2:00 p.m.   *It'll* begin boarding at 2:00 p.m.

3 Practice 3 [CD 1-22/DL 22]

下の文を読み、上の例文の太字の語句の中から適切なものを選び、空欄を埋めましょう。音声を聞いて答えをチェックしてみましょう。

Example: <u>You will</u> be late if you don't hurry up!

1. Can I please see the menu again? _____ like to order dessert.

2. I need to work more because _____ going to travel abroad next year.

3. Bring an umbrella because _____ probably rain this afternoon.

上で学習した発音を特に意識して、8頁の会話をペアの相手と練習してみましょう。

SPEAKING [Describing your routine in more detail]

1 Practice 1

下の、「頻度を表す副詞」と「接続詞」を使って、第1章(p.5)のPractice 2で完成させたYour daily routineを少し長めの文にまとめます。例にならって3つ作ってみましょう。できれば「朝食には〜を食べる」といった具体例も加えてみましょう。

「頻度を表す副詞」

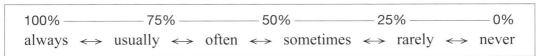

「接続詞」

| before / then / after / and / but / or / so / for / because / until / finally |

Example: I <u>always</u> wake up at 6:30 a.m. <u>and</u> <u>then</u> I usually take a shower.
I <u>often</u> eat breakfast at 7:10 a.m. <u>and</u> I <u>usually</u> eat toast and drink coffee.
I <u>usually</u> brush my teeth at 7:20 a.m. <u>after</u> I eat breakfast.

1. _____
2. _____
3. _____
4. _____

完成したら、ペアになって相手の人とお互いに文を読み合います。相手の人の文章を聴いて下の空欄に記入しましょう。この時、動詞に3人称単数形を使うように注意しましょう。

Example: (相手の名前) always wake**s** up at 6:30 a.m. and then he/she take**s** a shower.

1. _____
2. _____
3. _____
4. _____

PROVERBS AND SAYINGS

1 Practice 1 [CD 1–23/DL 23]

英語のことわざ（名言）を（必要に応じて）数回聴いて書き取ります。次にグループになって書き取ったものを比べてみます。もう一度音声を聴いて、必要があれば訂正しながらグループの答えを書きましょう。最終的に全員が正答にたどり着けるようにしましょう。

1. _____

   _____ (11 words)

2 Practice 2

グループ内でこのことわざ（名言）の意味について話し合ってa～cの中から正解を選びましょう。

a. The way to reach a goal is by working towards it.
b. The most important thing in life is to set difficult goals.
c. Travelling far distances can help us to reach our goals.

Useful phrases　この表現を使って話し合ってみよう

What did you hear?	What did you write?
What word did you write before ____?	What word did you write after ____?
How do you spell _____?	Look at my answer. Is anything missing?
What does ___ mean in Japanese?	What does this saying mean?

Chapter 3 ORIENTATION DAY
(University 1)

VOCABULARY PREVIEW

1 Pronunciation Practice [CD 1-24/DL 24]
英語の単語や表現を聞いて口頭で繰り返してください。

2 Dictation [CD 1-24/DL 24]
もう一度同じ単語や表現を聞き下の 1~8 番の空欄に記入しましょう。次にスペルが正しく書けているかどうか隣同士ペアになってチェックし合います。その際、下の囲み内の表現を使いながら英語で相談してみましょう。

> **Useful phrases**　この表現を使って話し合ってみよう
>
> What did you hear for number ~ ?　　How do you spell ~ ?
> I heard ~　　　　　　　　　　　　　I think it's spelled _ _ _ _ _

1. __adviser_____ (g)　　5. _____ (　)
2. _____ (　)　　6. _____ (　)
3. _____ (　)　　7. _____ (　)
4. _____ (　)　　8. _____ (　)

3 Definitions
3、4 人のグループを作ります。上の 8 つの単語や表現の定義として最もふさわしいものを下から選び、上のカッコ内に記号を記入しましょう。辞書は使わずにグループ内で英語で話し合って答えを選びます。その際、下の囲み内の表現を使ってみましょう。

a. a time when new students get information about the university
b. to continue on or to happen
c. the area and buildings around a university, college, etc.
d. something that is needed or required to do
e. to become used up or to come to an end
f. to enter or put information about something into a system
g. a person whose job is to give information or advice
h. colored liquid that is used for writing or printing

> **Useful phrases**　この表現を使って話し合ってみよう
>
> Are you ready? I'll read the definition and you choose the best word.
> What is ~ ?　　　　　　　　　　　I'm not sure. Maybe it is ~
> I think so too.　　　　　OR　　　I agree.
> I disagree. I think the answer is ~ .

SHORT DIALOG

まず右の頁の質問文に目を通してから会話文 (Part 1) を読みましょう。次に会話を聴いてそれぞれの質問に答えます。会話文の後半 (Part 2) は印刷されていませんので集中して聴きましょう。

> ***Situation***: Toshi is in Los Angeles. He is at the first information session for international students at his exchange university.

Part 1

[1] [CD 1–25/DL 25]

Director: Hello, my name is Sue Fisher and I am the Director of the International Student Center. It's nice to meet you all. Please take a few minutes to fill out your registration card for the International Student Orientation Session.

Toshi: I'm sorry Mrs. Fisher but I didn't get one. Where are they?

Director: Please call me Sue. There should be some on the table next to the entrance.

[2] [CD 1–26/DL 26]

Toshi: I just checked and there aren't any left on the table next to the door. I think you **must have** run out of cards.

Director: Thanks for letting me know. Don't worry though, I have some more in my bag. Let me go get some more … here you are.

Toshi: Thank you.

[3] [CD 1–27/DL 27]

Director: You **should have** received notice by email that the mandatory Orientation Session runs all day Friday and Saturday next weekend from 8 a.m. to 6 p.m. in the Student Center Building. After that, there will be a welcome party for you from 6:30 to 9:00 pm. in the cafeteria.

Jack: You will receive a timetable and maps of the campus, including instructions to get to the Student Center Building, at the end of the presentation.

Director: I'd like to introduce you all to Jack Taylor. He'll be your senior student adviser for orientation.

The conversation continues in Part 2.

Notes

director「所長、責任者」/ **fill out**「書き込む、記入する」/ **orientation session**「入学説明会、入学案内期間」/ **mandatory**「義務の、必須の」/ **instructions**「説明書き、指示」/ **senior**「上級の」

Question 1: What do the students need to fill out?

   A. An application form to work at the Student Center.
   B. A registration form for the orientation session.
   C. A special form to complete the course timetable.

Question 2: Why were there no cards on the table?

   A. Because Sue was late and had to run out to get some.
   B. Because students took them and they ran out of cards.
   C. Because Sue forget to put the cards on the table.

Question 3: What is Jack's job?

   A. He is the director of the student center.
   B. He is the senior student adviser.
   C. He is the leader of the presentation.

Part 2 [CD 1-28~30/DL 28~30]

Question 4: Toshi forgot to bring a pen.

     T   F

Question 5: Jack brought extra pens to the Orientation Session.

     T   F

Question 6: Toshi offers to help Jack with the Orientation Session.

     T   F

Notes

registration form「登録カード」／ **extra**「余分の、追加の」／ **just in case~**「~するといけないので、万が一~に備えて、念のために」／ **sorry to trouble you**「面倒をかけるね」

PRONUNCIATION　ポイント：① 音の連結による短縮形　② 弱母音の発音

> **ルール**：下のような語句を自然な速さで発音するとき、音同士の自然なつながりが起こり、完全に脱落してしまう音もあります。それぞれの最後の音は、"uh" や "ah" に近い音で弱母音と呼ばれるものです。従って下の例文のようにうしろに have が続くと、"uhv" と発音されることもあります。

1　Practice 1　[CD 1-31/DL 31]

音声の後に続けて発音してみましょう。

Must have	= Mustah	OR	Mustuhv
Could have	= Couldah	OR	Coulduhv
Should have	= Shouldah	OR	Shoulduhv
Would have	= Wouldah	OR	Woulduhv

2　Practice 2　[CD 1-32/DL 32]

音声を聞いて、下の例文を練習しましょう。まず、通常の発音での文が流れます。次に、音同士がつながった形の文が流れます。ペアの相手と両方の形の例文を発音してみましょう。

注記：下の例文のように、後ろに子音が続く場合は、"ah" もしくは "uhv" のといったくだけた発音がされます。一方、後ろに母音が続く場合は、その影響を受けて発音は "uhv" のみになります。

He **must have** failed the test.	= He *mustuhv* failed the test.
	OR　= He *mustah* failed the test.
I **could have** helped you study.	= I *coulduhv* helped you study.
	OR　= I *couldah* helped you study.
I **would have** if I'd thought of it.	= I *woulduhv* if I'd thought of it.

3　Practice 3　[CD 1-33/DL 33]

下の文を読み、上の例文の太字の語句の中から適切なものを選び、空欄を埋めましょう。音声を聞いて答えをチェックしてみましょう。

Example: I'm so hungry. I should have eaten breakfast.

1. I _____ studied if I had known we had a test.

2. I can't find my glasses. I _____ left them at home.

3. You _____ helped me carry the grocery bags. Half the food is yours!

上で学習した発音を特に意識して、14頁の会話をペアの相手と練習してみましょう。

SPEAKING [Filling Out Your Registration Card]

1 Practice 1

実際に自分で登録カードを記入してみましょう。完成したらペアになって、今度は下の表現を使って、相手の人に質問をしながらもう一つの登録カードを埋めていきましょう。

> **Useful Expressions**
>
> What's your name?   What's your nationality?   When were you born?
> What's your student ID number?   Where do you live?
> What's your phone number?   What's your email address?

My card:

```
          STUDENT ORIENTATION REGISTRATION CARD

   Name: _____
   Country of citizenship: _____
   Date of birth: _____
   Student identification number: _____
   Address: _____
            _____
   Telephone number: _____
   email: _____
```

My partner's card:

```
          STUDENT ORIENTATION REGISTRATION CARD

   Name: _____
   Country of citizenship: _____
   Date of birth: _____
   Student identification number: _____
   Address: _____
            _____
   Telephone number: _____
   email: _____
```

PROVERBS AND SAYINGS

1 Practice 1 [CD 1-34/DL 34]

英語のことわざ（名言）を（必要に応じて）数回聴いて書き取ります。次にグループになって書き取ったものを比べてみます。もう一度音声を聴いて、必要があれば訂正しながらグループの答えを書きましょう。最終的に全員が正答にたどり着けるようにしましょう。

1. _____ (15 words)

2 Practice 2

グループ内でこのことわざ（名言）の意味について話し合って a～c の中から正解を選びましょう。

A. The best way to learn something is by doing it.
B. The best way to learn something is by hearing it.
C. The best way to learn something is by reading it.

Useful phrases　この表現を使って話し合ってみよう

What did you hear?	What did you write?
What word did you write before ____?	What word did you write after ____?
How do you spell _____?	Look at my answer. Is anything missing?
What does ___ mean in Japanese?	What does this saying mean?

Chapter 4 CAREER ADVICE (University 2)

VOCABULARY PREVIEW

1 Pronunciation Practice [CD 1-35/DL 35]
英語の単語や表現を聞いて口頭で繰り返してください。

2 Dictation [CD 1-35/DL 35]
もう一度同じ単語や表現を聞き下の1~8番の空欄に記入しましょう。次にスペルが正しく書けているかどうか隣同士ペアになってチェックし合います。その際、下の囲み内の表現を使いながら英語で相談してみましょう。

> **Useful phrases**　この表現を使って話し合ってみよう
> What did you hear for number ~ ?　　How do you spell ~ ?
> I heard ~　　　　　　　　　　　　　I think it's spelled _ _ _ _ _

1. catering (f)　　　5. _____ ( )
2. _____ ( )　　6. _____ ( )
3. _____ ( )　　7. _____ ( )
4. _____ ( )　　8. _____ ( )

3 Definitions
3、4人のグループを作ります。上の8つの単語や表現の定義として最もふさわしいものを下から選び、上のカッコ内に記号を記入しましょう。辞書は使わずにグループ内で英語で話し合って答えを選びます。その際、下の囲み内の表現を使ってみましょう。

a. the main subject studied by a university student
b. areas of study (like history and literature) that give you general knowledge
c. relating to special skills needed to do a job or activity
d. the business that serves travelers and vacationers
e. to earn a degree from a school
f. the job of providing food and drinks for guests or customers at a party or meeting
g. suitable for use; reasonable for a particular situation
h. a person whose job is to give advice or guidance to people

> **Useful phrases**　この表現を使って話し合ってみよう
> Are you ready? I'll read the definition and you choose the best word.
> What is ~ ?　　　　　　　　　　I'm not sure. Maybe it is ~
> I think so too.　　　　　OR　　　I agree.
> I disagree. I think the answer is ~ .

SHORT DIALOG

まず右の頁の質問文に目を通してから会話文 (Part 1) を読みましょう。次に会話を聴いてそれぞれの質問に答えます。会話文の後半 (Part 2) は印刷されていませんので集中して聴きましょう。

Situation: Jack, a junior in university, is talking to a career counselor. He is asking questions about finding a job after graduation.

Part 1

[1] [CD 1–36/DL 36]

Counselor: Hi Jack. It's nice to **meet you**. I'm Sharon Smith, your career counselor. I understand that you have some questions.

Jack: Nice to meet you, too. I'm starting to think about job-hunting and would like to know what I can do to increase my chances of finding a good job after I graduate.

Counselor: It appears that the college major **that you** choose makes a difference. Unemployment and underemployment rates are quite different between different majors.

[2] [CD 1–37/DL 37]

Jack: What's the difference between unemployment and underemployment?

Counselor: Unemployment means not having a job at all. Underemployment means **that you** are working at a job that does not require a degree – you are over-qualified for the work you are doing.

Jack: So once I graduate from university, if I get a job making hamburgers I would be underemployed, right?

[3] [CD 1–38/DL 38]

Counselor: Well, yes and no. What's your major, Jack?

Jack: Business with a minor in Hospitality. What majors give students an advantage to finding a good job?

Counselor: Majors that give students technical training, like engineering or computers, or majors that focus on growing parts of the economy, such as education and health usually help students find work.

The conversation continues in Part 2.

Notes

junior「大学3年生」（主に米国）なお、それ以外の学年の呼び方は freshman「大学1年生」、sophomore「大学2年生」、senior「大学4年生」。/ **career**「職業、経歴」/ **job-hunting**「就職活動」/ **appear**「〜のようである」/ **make a difference**「違いが生じる」＝重要である、影響を及ぼす。/ **underemployment**「不完全雇用」能力以下の仕事に従事すること。/ **major**「専攻科目」/ **degree**「学位」

Question 1: What does the counselor say about finding a job after graduation?

A. The sooner you start your job hunt the better.
B. The college major that you choose will affect your job hunt.
C. Underemployment rates will affect your job hunt.

Question 2: What does the expression "underemployment" mean?

A. It means not having a job at all.
B. Working in a job that you are over-qualified for.
C. Working at a job making hamburgers.

Question 3: What majors help students most in finding a good job after graduation?

A. Hospitality and Economics
B. Engineering and Computers
C. Liberal Arts and Health

Part 2 [CD 1-39~41/DL 39~41]

Question 4: Jack wants to quit studying business and open a restaurant.

      T   F

Question 5: Ms. Smith recommends that Jack work in a restaurant.

      T   F

Question 6: Jack will most likely take Ms. Smith's advice.

      T   F

Notes ─────────────
over-qualified「資格過剰の」／ **engineering**「エンジニアリング、（建築・土木等の）工学」／ **catering business**「仕出し屋」／ **practical**「実用的な」／ **semester**「学期、セメスター」

PRONUNCIATION　ポイント：隣り合った音が同化して生まれる「ch」の音①

ルール：ある単語の末尾が「t」の音で終わり、かつ次に続く単語が「y（発音：/juː/）」で始まるとき、これら二つの単語が同化して「ch（発音：/tʃ/）」の音が生まれます。

1　Practice 1　[CD 1-42/DL 42]

音声の後に続けて発音してみましょう。

Meet you	= Meechu
That you	= Thatchu
Don't you	= Dontchu
What you	= Whatchu

2　Practice 2　[CD 1-43/DL 43]

音声を聞いて、下の例文を練習しましょう。まず、通常の発音での文が流れます。次に、音同士がつながった形の文が流れます。ペアの相手と両方の形の例文を発音してみましょう。

It's nice to **meet you**.	It's nice to *meechu*.
Why **don't you** try it?	Why *dontchu* try it?
That's **what you** should do.	That's *whatchu* should do.

3　Practice 3　[CD 1-44/DL 44]

下の文を読み、上の例文の太字の語句の中から適切なものを選び、空欄を埋めましょう。音声を聞いて答えをチェックしてみましょう。

Example: Do you think <u>that you</u> passed the test?

1. It's already 8:00 pm. _____ feel hungry?

2. I've wanted to _____ for so long.

3. I'm sorry, I didn't hear _____ said.

上で学習した発音を特に意識して、20頁の会話をペアの相手と練習してみましょう。

SPEAKING [Countries and nationalities]

1 Practice 1

隣同士でペアになります。下の四角内に世界のさまざまな国の名前を英語で書きなさい。制限時間は4分間です。出来るだけたくさん挙げてみましょう。

COUNTRIES OF THE WORLD

2 Practice 2

別のペアと向き合いましょう。それぞれのペアがリストアップした国名を一つずつ交互に読み上げていきます。自分たちのペアが挙げた国名が、相手ペアのリストに無ければ、1ポイント獲得です。自分たちのリストにない国名は書き加えましょう。両方のペアがリストアップしたすべての国名を読み切ったら終了です。ポイントの多い方の勝ち。双方のスコアを記入しましょう。

SCORE:　　　MY TEAM: _____　　　OTHER TEAM: _____

3 Practice 3

もう一度ペアに戻ります。下の表（Countryの項目下）に上のリストの国名を記入します。同様にその右隣の欄に、国籍の呼び方も記入してみましょう。

Country	Nationality	Country	Nationality
Japan	Japanese		

PROVERBS AND SAYINGS

1 Practice 1 [CD 1–45/DL 45]

英語のことわざ（名言）を（必要に応じて）数回聴いて書き取ります。次にグループになって書き取ったものを比べてみます。もう一度音声を聴いて、必要があれば訂正しながらグループの答えを書きましょう。最終的に全員が正答にたどり着けるようにしましょう。

1. _____

_____ (14 words)

2 Practice 2

グループ内でこのことわざ（名言）の意味について話し合って a～c の中から正解を選びましょう。

a. Most people will forget the things they learned in school.
b. We only become educated after we graduate from school.
c. Much of our education happens outside of the classroom.

Useful phrases この表現を使って話し合ってみよう
What did you hear? 　　　　　　　　　　What did you write?
What word did you write before ____?　 What word did you write after ____?
How do you spell ____?　　　　　　　　Look at my answer. Is anything missing?
What does ____ mean in Japanese?　　What does this saying mean?

Chapter 5 A WELCOME PARTY

(Friends 1)

VOCABULARY PREVIEW

1 Pronunciation Practice [CD 1–46/DL 46]

英語の単語や表現を聞いて口頭で繰り返してください。

2 Dictation [CD 1–46/DL 46]

もう一度同じ単語や表現を聞き下の1~8番の空欄に記入しましょう。次にスペルが正しく書けているかどうか隣同士ペアになってチェックし合います。その際、下の囲み内の表現を使いながら英語で相談してみましょう。

> **Useful phrases**　この表現を使って話し合ってみよう
>
> What did you hear for number ~ ?　　How do you spell ~ ?
> I heard ~　　　　　　　　　　　　　I think it's spelled _ _ _ _ _

1. at home_____ (b)　5. _____ (   )
2. _____ (   )　　　　　6. _____ (   )
3. _____ (   )　　　　　7. _____ (   )
4. _____ (   )　　　　　8. _____ (   )

3 Definitions

3、4人のグループを作ります。上の8つの単語や表現の定義として最もふさわしいものを下から選び、上のカッコ内に記号を記入しましょう。辞書は使わずにグループ内で英語で話し合って答えを選びます。その際、下の囲み内の表現を使ってみましょう。

a. an expression that means "start eating and drinking"
b. feeling relaxed and comfortable
c. to take something with the promise of giving it back
d. a building on a school campus where students can live
e. doing and seeing things and having things happen to you
f. a group of people who will graduate in the same year
g. to make something better
h. the feeling when you cannot understand a thing clearly

> **Useful phrases**　この表現を使って話し合ってみよう
>
> Are you ready? I'll read the definition and you choose the best word.
> What is ~ ?　　　　　　　　　I'm not sure. Maybe it is ~
> I think so too.　　　　OR　　I agree.
> I disagree. I think the answer is ~ .

SHORT DIALOG

まず右の頁の質問文に目を通してから会話文 (Part 1) を読みましょう。次に会話を聴いてそれぞれの質問に答えます。会話文の後半 (Part 2) は印刷されていませんので集中して聴きましょう。

> ***Situation***: Toshi is at the Orientation Session Party. He is meeting the other international students.

Part 1

[1] [CD 1–47/DL 47]

Director: Welcome to this year's cohort of international students. I hope this year offers you many new experiences. If there is anything you need or have any questions, visit my office or talk to Jack, your senior adviser.

Jack: I will live in the International House dormitory with you all this year. I'm here to help so don't be shy if you have any questions.

Director: Thank you Jack. **Could you** all please get something to drink?

[2] [CD 1–48/DL 48]

Jack: There is plenty to eat and drink so dig in! Ready? Cheers!

Toshi: Cheers! (*Toshi thinking out loud to himself*) There are so many people I don't know. How will I ever make friends?

Jack: Hey! What **did you** say your name was? You're the one who borrowed the pen.

[3] [CD 1–49/DL 49]

Toshi: Oh no! I forgot to return it. How stupid of me. I'm Toshi. I'm from Japan.

Jack: Don't worry about it. With everything in English you must feel confused.

Toshi: Yeah, a bit but I'm so excited to be here. Studying abroad is my dream come true. And **would you** believe that my sister lives here? Now I can visit her anytime!

The conversation continues in Part 2.

Notes

cohort「仲間、グループ」/ **offer**「提供する、用意する」/ **dormitory** "dorm" という略語もよく使われる。/ **plenty**「たくさん（の）」

Question 1: What should students who have questions do?

A. They should live in International House.
B. They should visit the director's office.
C. They should talk to international students.

Question 2: What does Jack tell the students about the food and drink?

A. He tells them to wait to eat but to drink now.
B. He tells them to wait to drink but to eat now.
C. He tells them to begin to eat and drink now.

Question 3: Why does Jack say that Toshi must feel confused?

A. Because Toshi forgot to return the pen.
B. Because Toshi is worried about things.
C. Because Toshi has to do everything in English.

Part 2 [CD 1-50~52/DL 50~52]

Question 4: Jack wants to make the international students feel welcome.

T   F

Question 5: Jack and Toshi will both live in the dormitory.

T   F

Question 6: Candy made up an English name to help people who can speak Chinese.

T   F

PRONUNCIATION   ポイント：隣り合った音が同化して生まれる「j」(/ʤ/) の音

> **ルール**：ある単語の末尾が「d」の音で終わり、かつ次に続く単語が「y（発音：/juː/）」で始まるとき、これら二つの単語を結ぶ「j（発音：/ʤ/）」の音が生まれます。この結果、例えば「you」という単語は、「ya」という発音に短縮されます。

1 Practice 1   [CD 1–53/DL 53]

音声の後に続けて発音してみましょう。

Did you	= Didjya
Could you	= Couldjya
Would you	= Wouldjya

2 Practice 2   [CD 1–54/DL 54]

音声を聞いて、下の例文を練習しましょう。まず、通常の発音での文が流れます。次に、音同士がつながった形の文が流れます。ペアの相手と両方の形の例文を発音してみましょう。

Could you please get something to drink?　　*Couldjya* please get something to drink?
What **did you** say your name was?　　　　　What *didjya* say your name was?
　　　　　　　　　　　　　　　　　OR　　 *Whad-jya* say your name was?
Would you believe she lives here?　　　　　 *Wouldjya* believe she lives here?

3 Practice 3   [CD 1–55/DL 55]

下の文を読み、上の例文の太字の語句の中から適切なものを選び、空欄を埋めましょう。音声を聞いて答えをチェックしてみましょう。

Example: What <u>would you</u> do with one million dollars?

1. What happened to the cake I baked? _____ eat it all?

2. I feel a little cold. _____ close the door please?

3. Excuse me but _____ mind passing me that book?

上で学習した発音を特に意識して、26頁の会話をペアの相手と練習してみましょう。

SPEAKING [At a party]

1 Practice 1

面識の無い人が大勢いるパーティー会場にいると想像してみましょう。今、相手のことをよく知るために、クラスの中で下の1~15の項目にあてはまる人を見つけて、その人の名前を空欄に記入していきましょう。その際、下の例のような表現を使って出来るだけ多くの人と英語で話し合って複数の人の名前を入れるように努力してみましょう。

Example:

Q. Have you (ever) eaten raw fish?
A. Yes, I have. I've eaten sushi.   OR   No, I haven't.   It sounds 形容詞！

「形容詞例」

dangerous / difficult / terrible / fun / exciting / interesting

Find someone who …

1. _____ has had a pet.
2. _____ has driven a car.
3. _____ has flown a kite.
4. _____ has gone skiing.
5. _____ has fallen in love.
6. _____ has gone surfing.
7. _____ has broken a bone.
8. _____ has lost his/her wallet.
9. _____ has been to Hawaii.
10. _____ has touched a snake.
11. _____ has cheated on a test.
12. _____ has done volunteer work.
13. _____ has eaten a very strange food.
14. _____ has made dinner for their family.
15. _____ has seen or met a famous person.

How many different names did you write down? _____

PROVERBS AND SAYINGS

1 Practice 1 [CD 1-56/DL 56]

英語のことわざ（名言）を（必要に応じて）数回聴いて書き取ります。次にグループになって書き取ったものを比べてみます。もう一度音声を聴いて、必要があれば訂正しながらグループの答えを書きましょう。最終的に全員が正答にたどり着けるようにしましょう。

1. _____

_____ (12 words)

2 Practice 2

グループ内でこのことわざ（名言）の意味について話し合って a～c の中から正解を選びましょう。

a. You should not disturb friends past midnight.
b. Our true friends will help us at anytime.
c. It doesn't matter what time it is when you call friends.

Useful phrases この表現を使って話し合ってみよう

What did you hear?	What did you write?
What word did you write before ____?	What word did you write after ____?
How do you spell ____?	Look at my answer. Is anything missing?
What does ___ mean in Japanese?	What does this saying mean?

Chapter 6　BREAK A LEG!

(Friends 2)

VOCABULARY PREVIEW

1　Pronunciation Practice　[CD 1-57/DL 57]
英語の単語や表現を聞いて口頭で繰り返してください。

2　Dictation　[CD 1-57/DL 57]
もう一度同じ単語や表現を聞き下の1~8番の空欄に記入しましょう。次にスペルが正しく書けているかどうか隣同士ペアになってチェックし合います。その際、下の囲み内の表現を使いながら英語で相談してみましょう。

> **Useful phrases**　この表現を使って話し合ってみよう
> What did you hear for number ~ ?　　How do you spell ~ ?
> I heard ~　　　　　　　　　　　　　I think it's spelled _ _ _ _ _

1. crowd_____ (e)　　5. _____ ( )
2. _____ ( )　　　　　　6. _____ ( )
3. _____ ( )　　　　　　7. _____ ( )
4. _____ ( )　　　　　　8. _____ ( )

3　Definitions
3、4人のグループを作ります。上の8つの単語や表現の定義として最もふさわしいものを下から選び、上のカッコ内に記号を記入しましょう。辞書は使わずにグループ内で英語で話し合って答えを選びます。その際、下の囲み内の表現を使ってみましょう。

a. working fewer hours than is considered standard
b. a group of people who work for an organization or business
c. a situation that needs attention right away
d. very quickly in usually an unexpected way
e. a large group of people who are together in one place
f. a word or phrase
g. the parts of a piece of music that we sing
h. almost not at all

> **Useful phrases**　この表現を使って話し合ってみよう
> Are you ready? I'll read the definition and you choose the best word.
> What is ~ ?　　　　　　　　　　I'm not sure. Maybe it is ~
> I think so too.　　　　　OR　　　I agree.
> I disagree. I think the answer is ~ .

SHORT DIALOG

まず右の頁の質問文に目を通してから会話文 (Part 1) を読みましょう。次に会話を聴いてそれぞれの質問に答えます。会話文の後半 (Part 2) は印刷されていませんので集中して聴きましょう。

> *Situation*: Toshi and Jack are talking about the coming weekend. Toshi's band will perform at the school festival but Jack has to work.

Part 1

[1] [CD 1–58/DL 58]

Toshi: Are you **going to** go to the school festival this weekend?

Jack: No, I **want to** go but I can't. Two part-time staff suddenly quit last week. My boss asked me to go in so I've **got to** work. It's an emergency and I can use the money.

Toshi: That's too bad. There are some good bands playing. As a matter of fact, my band is playing!

[2] [CD 1–59/DL 59]

Jack: Really? I've heard that your band is pretty good. Too bad I can't go. I hope you get a good crowd out to hear you. Break a leg!

Toshi: Are you kidding me? Break a leg! What do you mean?

Jack: Oh! I'm sorry Toshi, it means "good luck". I don't *really* hope that you break any bones, just play some good music!

[3] [CD 1–60/DL 60]

Toshi: Ah, I see. There is an expression in Japanese when we want to say good luck – *ganbatte*. You hear it all the time.

Jack: And does it mean you're telling someone to break a leg, too?

Toshi: No, it actually means something like "don't give up" or "hang in there". Lots of Japanese people like to give their best effort.

The conversation continues in Part 2.

Notes

quit「(仕事や習慣を) やめる」／ **as a matter of fact**「実は、実を言うと」／ **crowd**「聴衆、観客」／ **bone**「骨」／ **hang in there**「(粘り強く) がんばって」通常励ましの意で命令形で使われる。(その場で踏ん張れ、踏みとどまれ) が元来の意味。

Question 1: Why does Jack's boss need him to work?

A. Because he wants to attend the school festival.
B. Because an emergency came up at home.
C. Because two other workers suddenly quit.

Question 2: What does the expression "break a leg" mean?

A. Break your bone!
B. Good luck!
C. Slow down!

Question 3: How can we explain the expression *ganbatte* in English?

A. Break your leg!
B. Don't give up!
C. Hang around!

Part 2 [CD 1–61~63/DL 61~63]

Question 4: Toshi sings in his new band.

      T   F

Question 5: Toshi did not work part-time in Japan.

      T   F

Question 6: According to Toshi, most Japanese university students work full-time during the summer vacation.

      T   F

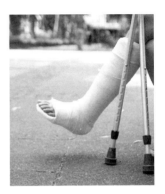

Notes ─────
~ **to come up**「〜が（急に）起きる」／ **work part-time**「パートタイム（時間給）で働く」

Chapter 6 BREAK A LEG (Friends 2)

PRONUNCIATION　ポイント：① 音の連結と脱落　② 弱母音の発音 [ə]

> ルール：自然な速さでの発音の場合、「going to」「want to」「have to」あるいは「got to」「ought to」といった語句に動詞が続く場合、語尾が縮まり、弱母音 [ə] の発音になります。

1 Practice 1　[CD 1–64/DL 64]

音声の後に続けて発音してみましょう。

Going to	= Gonna
Want to	= Wanna
Got to	= Gotta
Have to	= Hafta
Ought to	= Oughta

2 Practice 2　[CD 1–65/DL 65]

音声を聞いて、下の例文を練習しましょう。まず、通常の発音での文が流れます。次に、音同士がつながった形の文が流れます。ペアの相手と両方の形の例文を発音してみましょう。

Are you **going to** go to the festival?　　Are you *gonna* go to the festival?
I really **want to** go but I can't.　　I really *wanna* go but I can't.
I **have to** work.　　I *hafta* work.

3 Practice 3　[CD 1–66/DL 66]

下の文を読み、上の例文の太字の語句の中から適切なものを選び、空欄を埋めましょう。音声を聞いて答えをチェックしてみましょう。

Example: Do you want to go to the concert with me?

1. Are you _____ go to the party?

2. I can't, I _____ study.

3. I _____ go but I'm busy.

上で学習した発音を特に意識して、32 頁の会話をペアの相手と練習してみましょう。

SPEAKING [My plans and goals]

1 Practice 1

PRONUNCIATION (p. 34) で学習したすべての表現を使って、自分のことについて文を5つ書いてみましょう。

Example:

I **want to** travel all over the world after I graduate.
I'm **going to** study English every day starting today.
In my 3rd year of university I **have to** start job-hunting.

1. _____
2. _____
3. _____
4. _____
5. _____

ペアになって自分の書いた文をお互いに相手に読んでみましょう。
下の空欄に、相手の人からの情報を記入していきましょう。その際、動詞を3人称単数形に変えることを忘れないようにしましょう。

Example: (Mariko) is going to study Spanish.
        (Mariko) want**s** to travel all over the world after she graduates.

1. _____
2. _____
3. _____
4. _____
5. _____

註：上記2番目の例の様に3人称単数形が使われ、一般動詞の語尾に "s" が付いたり、あるいは "has to" が使われる時は以下のような音の変化が起こります。

　　例） wants to　→　wansta
　　　　 has to　　→　hasta

Chapter 6 BREAK A LEG (Friends 2)

PROVERBS AND SAYINGS

1 Practice 1 [CD 1–67/DL 67]

英語のことわざ（名言）を（必要に応じて）数回聴いて書き取ります。次にグループになって書き取ったものを比べてみます。もう一度音声を聴いて、必要があれば訂正しながらグループの答えを書きましょう。最終的に全員が正答にたどり着けるようにしましょう。

1. _____ (6 words)

2 Practice 2

グループ内でこのことわざ（名言）の意味について話し合ってa～cの中から正解を選びましょう。

a. Birds are similar to people, they gather in groups.
b. Friends will fly away like birds if you are not kind.
c. People who are similar often gather together.

Useful phrases   この表現を使って話し合ってみよう

What did you hear?	What did you write?
What word did you write before ____?	What word did you write after ____?
How do you spell _____?	Look at my answer. Is anything missing?
What does ___ mean in Japanese?	What does this saying mean?

Chapter 7 A SPECIAL INVITATION
(Family 1)

VOCABULARY PREVIEW

1 Pronunciation Practice [CD 1-68/DL 68]
英語の単語や表現を聞いて口頭で繰り返してください。

2 Dictation [CD 1-68/DL 68]
もう一度同じ単語や表現を聞き下の1~8番の空欄に記入しましょう。次にスペルが正しく書けているかどうか隣同士ペアになってチェックし合います。その際、下の囲み内の表現を使いながら英語で相談してみましょう。

> **Useful phrases**　この表現を使って話し合ってみよう
> What did you hear for number ~ ?　　How do you spell ~ ?
> I heard ~　　　　　　　　　　　　　I think it's spelled _ _ _ _ _

1. __bridal registry__ (e)　　5. _____ (　)
2. _____ (　)　　　　　　　6. _____ (　)
3. _____ (　)　　　　　　　7. _____ (　)
4. _____ (　)　　　　　　　8. _____ (　)

3 Definitions
3、4人のグループを作ります。上の8つの単語や表現の定義として最もふさわしいものを下から選び、上のカッコ内に記号を記入しましょう。辞書は使わずにグループ内で英語で話し合って答えを選びます。その際、下の囲み内の表現を使ってみましょう。

a. a formal event that is part of a social or religious occasion
b. a man that a woman is engaged to be married to.
c. (something) done in the same way for a very long time.
d. a member of your family.
e. a list of gifts that a couple to be married wants to receive.
f. an event where two people get married to each other.
g. plates, bowls and cups that are made of baked clay and are usually white.
h. a party to celebrate or welcome someone or something.

> **Useful phrases**　この表現を使って話し合ってみよう
> Are you ready? I'll read the definition and you choose the best word.
> What is ~ ?　　　　　　　　　　　　I'm not sure. Maybe it is ~
> I think so too.　　　　　　OR　　　I agree.
> I disagree. I think the answer is ~ .

SHORT DIALOG

まず右の頁の質問文に目を通してから会話文 (Part 1) を読みましょう。次に会話を聴いてそれぞれの質問に答えます。会話文の後半 (Part 2) は印刷されていませんので集中して聴きましょう。

Situation: Jack's sister will get married next weekend. Jack has decided to invite Toshi to the party that takes place after the wedding.

Part 1

[1] [CD 1-69/DL 69]

Toshi: Jack: Hey Toshi, what are you doing this weekend?
Toshi: I **do not** have any plans, why?
Jack: Well, my older sister Donna is getting married in my hometown. Do you want to come to the wedding reception with me? **It will** be a lot of fun!

[2] [CD 1-70/DL 70]

Toshi: Well, I'd love to go but I **do not** have a suit.
Jack: Oh, **do not** worry about that. You **do not** have to attend the wedding. Just come with me to the party afterwards. You can meet my family.
Toshi: Well that does sound like a lot of fun. What kind of gift should I bring?

[3] [CD 1-71/DL 71]

Jack: **It is** usually a practical gift; something the couple can use at home.
Toshi: In Japan people give money. It helps them to pay for the wedding and they can buy things they need.
Jack: Traditionally the couple prepares a bridal registry with a list of gifts, like pots and pans, or chinaware that they'd like to receive. Money is becoming more common.

The conversation continues in Part 2.

Notes

afterwards「後で」／ **bridal registry**「ブライダル・レジストリ（結婚贈答品登録リスト）」結婚を控えたカップルが、結婚祝いとして欲しい品物のリストを作成し、それをもとに友人などが贈り物を決める仕組み。現代では結婚予定カップルによるリストの作成や、贈り主側によるリストの確認と品物の注文まで、インターネットで行われるのが主流になってきている。／ **pot**「(底の深い) なべ」／ **pan**「浅いなべ、フライパン」

Question 1: What does Jack ask Toshi to do?

   A. He asks Toshi to meet his sister.
   B. He wants Toshi to see his hometown.
   C. He invites him to go to a party.

Question 2: Does Toshi need to wear a suit?

   A. Yes, he must wear a suit for the wedding.
   B. Yes, he must wear a suit for the reception.
   C. No, he does not need to wear a suit.

Question 3: What are some traditional wedding gifts in the USA?

   A. Money to pay for the wedding.
   B. A bridal registry with a list.
   C. Useful items for the house.

Part 2 [CD 1–72~74/DL 72~74]

Question 4: The reception is for both friends and family.

   T   F

Question 5: Toshi must prepare a speech to give at the party.

   T   F

Question 6: Toshi is a little nervous about going to the reception.

   T   F

Notes ─────────
   relatives「親戚」／ **informal** くだけた、形式張らない／ **on top of that**「おまけに、それに加えて」

Chapter 7 A SPECIAL INVITATION (Family 1)

PRONUNCIATION　ポイント：短縮形の発音時の母音の脱落 ②

> **ルール**：下のような語句を自然な速さで発音するとき、音同士のつながりが起こり、完全に脱落する母音があります。

1　Practice 1　[CD 1-75/DL 75]

音声の後に続けて発音してみましょう。

Do not	Don't
It will	It'll
It is	It's
Is not	Isn't

2　Practice 2　[CD 1-76/DL 76]

音声を聞いて、下の例文を練習しましょう。まず、通常の発音での文が流れます。次に、音同士がつながった形の文が流れます。ペアの相手と両方の形の例文を発音してみましょう。

I **do not** have any plans.	I *don't* have any plans.
It will be a lot of fun.	*It'll* be a lot of fun.
It is a lot of fun.	*It's* a lot of fun.
My English **is not** very good yet.	My English *isn't* very good yet.

3　Practice 3　[CD 1-77/DL 77]

下の文を読み、上の例文の太字の語句の中から適切なものを選び、空欄を埋めましょう。音声を聞いて答えをチェックしてみましょう。

Example: <u>Do not</u> worry, you'll do fine.

1. Don't leave, the party _____ over yet.

2. I _____ understand what you said.

3. Bring a jacket, _____ supposed to get cool tonight.

上で学習した発音を特に意識して、38 頁の会話をペアの相手と練習してみましょう。

SPEAKING [Making a bridal registry list]

1 Practice 1

あなたは結婚を目前に控えていると想像してみましょう。まず自分が欲しい品物の10項目を下のブライダル・レジストリのリストに挙げましょう。次にペアの相手とリストを比べてから、もう2〜5項目を追加します。その際、何の役に立つのか等、選んだ理由も書きましょう。最後に3〜4人のグループになって、リストの項目や選んだ理由について話し合ってみましょう。

Useful phrases　下の表現を使って話し合ってみよう

I want to get a/an/some _____.

Why do you want to get a/an/some _____?

I want a/an because _____.

How can you use a/an _____?

We can use it to (+ simple verb) _____.

We can use it for (+ verb+ing) _____.

Bridal Registry Gift List

_____
_____
_____
_____
_____
_____
_____
_____

Reasons: _____
_____
_____
_____
_____

PROVERBS AND SAYINGS

1 **Practice 1** [CD 1-78/DL 78]

英語のことわざ（名言）を（必要に応じて）数回聴いて書き取ります。次にグループになって書き取ったものを比べてみます。もう一度音声を聴いて、必要があれば訂正しながらグループの答えを書きましょう。最終的に全員が正答にたどり着けるようにしましょう。

1. _____ (9 words)

2 **Practice 2**

グループ内でこのことわざ（名言）の意味について話し合ってa～cの中から正解を選びましょう。

a. A person's work is more important than their family.
b. A person's family is more important than their work.
c. A person should never do business with family members.

Useful phrases この表現を使って話し合ってみよう

What did you hear?	What did you write?
What word did you write before ____?	What word did you write after ____?
How do you spell ____?	Look at my answer. Is anything missing?
What does ___ mean in Japanese?	What does this saying mean?

---

42 SOUNDS REAL!

Chapter 8 A WEDDING RECEPTION
(Family 2)

VOCABULARY PREVIEW

1 Pronunciation Practice [CD 1-79/DL 79]
英語の単語や表現を聞いて口頭で繰り返してください。

2 Dictation [CD 1-79/DL 79]
もう一度同じ単語や表現を聞き下の 1~8 番の空欄に記入しましょう。次にスペルが正しく書けているかどうか隣同士ペアになってチェックし合います。その際、下の囲み内の表現を使いながら英語で相談してみましょう。

> **Useful phrases**　この表現を使って話し合ってみよう
> What did you hear for number ~ ?　　How do you spell ~ ?
> I heard ~　　　　　　　　　　　　　I think it's spelled _ _ _ _ _

1. __bride_____ (g)　　5. _____ (   )
2. _____ (   )　　6. _____ (   )
3. _____ (   )　　7. _____ (   )
4. _____ (   )　　8. _____ (   )

3 Definitions
3、4人のグループを作ります。上の8つの単語や表現の定義として最もふさわしいものを下から選び、上のカッコ内に記号を記入しましょう。辞書は使わずにグループ内で英語で話し合って答えを選びます。その際、下の囲み内の表現を使ってみましょう。

a. an unusual or strange person
b. to get along well
c. a brother or a sister
d. a man who has just married or is about to be married
e. a senior student whose job is to live in the dormitory to help younger students
f. to present someone to another person by their name
g. a woman who has just married or is about to be married
h. a soft and sweet candy made with sugar, butter and milk

> **Useful phrases**　この表現を使って話し合ってみよう
> Are you ready? I'll read the definition and you choose the best word.
> What is ~ ?　　　　　　　　　　I'm not sure. Maybe it is ~
> I think so too.　　　　OR　　　　I agree.
> I disagree. I think the answer is ~ .

SHORT DIALOG

まず右の頁の質問文に目を通してから会話文 (Part 1) を読みましょう。次に会話を聴いてそれぞれの質問に答えます。会話文の後半 (Part 2) は印刷されていませんので集中して聴きましょう。

Situation: Toshi is at the wedding reception and is meeting some of the people who are there.

Part 1

[1] [CD 1–80/DL 80]

Jenny: Hi there! Are you having a good time?

Toshi: Yes, I've met so many people but I can't seem to remember anyone's name! By the way, I'm Toshi but you can call me Tom if it's hard for you to remember. I'm from Japan. Do you know the bride or the groom?

Jenny: So you're Toshi! I've heard a lot about you. I'm Jenny.

[2] [CD 1–81/DL 81]

Toshi: You're Jenny? Jack told me he had an older sister named Jenny.

Jenny: I knew that Jack had a friend from Japan but he never told me how you two met.

Toshi: Well, Jack was my student adviser for the international student orientation. He is also the R.A. in the International House dormitory.

[3] [CD 1–82/DL 82]

Jenny: Yeah, that sounds like Jack. He is a really great guy, always helping people out.

Toshi: I don't know what I would **do if** I hadn't met him. He has introduced me to so many people on campus. We **do a** lot of fun things together, too.

Jenny: Who have you met at the reception today?

The conversation continues in Part 2.

Notes

R.A. = Resident Assistant「寮長」通常、学生が大学当局による選考を経て有給で務める。

Question 1: Why does Jenny say "So you're Toshi!"?

A. Because she wants him to check her pronunciation.
B. Because she wants to remember his name so she repeats it.
C. Because she has already heard about him somehow.

Question 2: Where does Jack live while he is in university?

A. At home with his family.
B. In the university dormitory.
C. In an apartment by himself.

Question 3: Why does Jenny say "Yeah, that sounds like Jack"?

A. Because Jack is nearby and she can hear his voice.
B. Because Toshi and Jack's voices sound very similar.
C. Because Toshi's description of Jack sounds correct to her.

Part 2 [CD 1–83~85/DL 83~85]

Question 4: Jeff is Jenny's brother-in-law.

   T F

Question 5: Jenny has been working in advertising since last year.

   T F

Question 6: Jack says that Toshi will like all the guests at the party.

   T F

Notes

have trouble ~ing「〜するのに苦労する」／ **advertising**「広告（の）」／ **cousin**「いとこ」

Chapter 8 A WEDDING RECEPTION (Family 2)

PRONUNCIATION　ポイント：母音同士のつながりによる子音の発生

> ルール：自然な速さでの発音の場合、母音の /uː/（例：do）や /oʊ/（例：go）に別の母音が続くとき、音の連結が起こり、子音の /w/ の音が生まれます。

1 Practice 1 [CD 1–86/DL 86]

音声の後に続けて発音してみましょう。

Do if　　　　= Doowif
Do a　　　　= Doowa
Go and　　　= Gowand
Go over　　　= Gowover

2 Practice 2 [CD 1–87/DL 87]

音声を聞いて、下の例文を練習しましょう。まず、通常の発音での文が流れます。次に、音同士がつながった形の文が流れます。ペアの相手と両方の形の例文を発音してみましょう。

We **do a** lot of fun things.　　　　　We *doowa* lot of fun things.
I'll let you **go and** talk to him.　　　I'll let you *gowand* talk to him.
Let's **go over** there.　　　　　　　 Let's *gowover* there.

3 Practice 3 [CD 1–88/DL 88]

下の文を読み、上の例文の太字の語句の中から適切なものを選び、空欄を埋めましょう。音声を聞いて答えをチェックしてみましょう。

Example: She looked too young to drive <u>so I</u> asked her how old she was.

1. My basketball coach taught me how to _____ jump shot.

2. Mom wants us to _____ to the store to buy some bread.

3. I want you to _____ do your homework right now!

上で学習した発音を特に意識して、44頁の会話をペアの相手と練習してみましょう。

SPEAKING   [Your family]

1 Practice 1

下の表に、自分の家族や親せきについての情報を記入しましょう。

Relationship	Name and (approximate) age
Me	
Parents, brothers, sisters (siblings)	
Grandparents, great-grandparents	
Aunts, uncles, cousins	
Other (in-laws, etc.)	

2 Practice 2

次に、ペアを組んで、相手の人から家族や親せきの情報を聞いて次の表に記入していきましょう。その際、下の囲み内の表現を使いながら質問をし合いましょう。

Relationship	Name and (approximate) age
My partner	
Parents, brothers, sisters (siblings)	
Grandparents, great-grandparents	
Aunts, uncles, cousins	
Other (in-laws, etc.)	

Useful Expressions

What's your name? How old are you?
What's your _____'s name? How old is he/she?

My father's name is _____ and he is (around) ____ years old.
I don't have a sister.

Chapter 8 A WEDDING RECEPTION (Family 2)

PROVERBS AND SAYINGS

1 Practice 1 [CD 1-89/DL 89]

英語のことわざ（名言）を（必要に応じて）数回聴いて書き取ります。次にグループになって書き取ったものを比べてみます。もう一度音声を聴いて、必要があれば訂正しながらグループの答えを書きましょう。最終的に全員が正答にたどり着けるようにしましょう。

1. _____

_____ (10 words)

2 Practice 2

グループ内でこのことわざ（名言）の意味について話し合ってa～cの中から正解を選びましょう。

a. Most people in a family are kind but some are a little strange.
b. Family will give us not only sweet but also bitter memories.
c. If parents treat children too kindly they will not grow strong.

Useful phrases　この表現を使って話し合ってみよう

What did you hear?	What did you write?
What word did you write before ____?	What word did you write after ____?
How do you spell ____?	Look at my answer. Is anything missing?
What does ____ mean in Japanese?	What does this saying mean?

Chapter 9 A TEXT MESSAGE
(Relationships 1)

VOCABULARY PREVIEW

1 Pronunciation Practice [CD 2-1/DL 90]

英語の単語や表現を聞いて口頭で繰り返してください。

2 Dictation [CD 2-1/DL 90]

もう一度同じ単語や表現を聞き下の 1~8 番の空欄に記入しましょう。次にスペルが正しく書けているかどうか隣同士ペアになってチェックし合います。その際、下の囲み内の表現を使いながら英語で相談してみましょう。

> *Useful phrases*　この表現を使って話し合ってみよう
> What did you hear for number ~ ?　　How do you spell ~ ?
> I heard ~　　　　　　　　　　　　　I think it's spelled _ _ _ _ _

1. __ASAP_____ (b)　　5. _____ ( )
2. _____ ( )　　　　6. _____ ( )
3. _____ ( )　　　　7. _____ ( )
4. _____ ( )　　　　8. _____ ( )

3 Definitions

3、4 人のグループを作ります。上の 8 つの単語や表現の定義として最もふさわしいものを下から選び、上のカッコ内に記号を記入しましょう。辞書は使わずにグループ内で英語で話し合って答えを選びます。その際、下の囲み内の表現を使ってみましょう。

a. having a large amount of something
b. happening without delay, as soon as possible
c. to get or take something in a quick or informal way
d. slang for coffee
e. a good friend
f. a small amount of food eaten between meals
g. a child of your uncle or aunt
h. not long ago

> *Useful phrases*　この表現を使って話し合ってみよう
> Are you ready? I'll read the definition and you choose the best word.
> What is ~ ?　　　　　　　　　　I'm not sure. Maybe it is ~
> I think so too.　　　　　OR　　　I agree.
> I disagree. I think the answer is ~ .

SHORT DIALOG

まず右の頁の質問文に目を通してから会話文 (Part 1) を読みましょう。次に会話を聴いてそれぞれの質問に答えます。会話文の後半 (Part 2) は印刷されていませんので集中して聴きましょう。

Situation: Jack is meeting friends for coffee and a movie. He wants Toshi to come so he can introduce him to someone new.

Part 1

[1] [CD 2–2/DL 91]

Jack: Hey Toshi, there you are! I've been looking for you. I wanted to ask you if you want to come to the movies tonight?

Toshi: Sure Jack, I'd love to go! Will it be a large group or something smaller?

Jack: Just a few of us. My buddy Joshua will be there. Actually, he introduced me to Laura.

[2] [CD 2–3/DL 92]

Toshi: What time is everyone meeting?

Jack: Well, the movie starts at 9:30 but we're planning on getting together a little earlier to grab a snack. Text me later if you can join us. I will let you know where we are.

Toshi: OK. I have some studying to do today but I will let you know when I finish.

[3] [CD 2–4/DL 93]

(Toshi finishes studying for the day and sends a text message to Jack)

Toshi (texts): Hi Jack, I've been studying for hours and I'm ready for a break. Where are you?

Jack (texts): **GR8** We're @ Java Hut come **ASAP** wanna introduce **U2** Joshua **CU L8R**

Toshi (texts): Can you please explain your text? I don't know what you're trying to say.

The conversation continues in Part 2.

Notes

buddy「仲間、友達、相棒」米英語で友人を表すくだけた表現。「おい」「お前」「兄弟」などの呼びかけの意味でも使われる。／ **grab**「(手早く) 食べる・飲む、つかむ」／ **text**（書かれた）文字、文章

50　SOUNDS REAL!

Question 1: Why has Jack been looking for Toshi?

   A. He wants to ask him for some help tonight.
   B. He wants to ask him to go out with him tonight.
   C. He wants to ask him to move some things.

Question 2: What time will Jack and his friends meet?

   A. They'll meet at 9:30 outside the theatre.
   B. They'll meet before the movie to eat something.
   C. They'll meet early to study together.

Question 3: Why does Toshi have trouble reading Jack's message?

   A. Because he is tired from studying for hours.
   B. Because Toshi can't read English very well yet.
   C. Because Jack uses special text language.

Part 2 [CD 2-5~7/DL 94~96]

(*Jack and Toshi exchange one more text message.*)

Question 4: Toshi will go to meet Jack and his friends right away.

     T   F

(*The conversation continues.*)

Question 5: This is the first time for Toshi to meet Laura.

     T   F

Question 6: Toshi wants to get something to drink before going to the theater.

     T   F

Notes ————————
   What do you say we ~ (≒ How about we ~)「～しましょうか」

PRONUNCIATION　ポイント：通信 (SNS) 用の略語を使った簡潔な表現

現代の若者の間では、メールやチャットで親しい友人などとメッセージをやり取りする時は、文字数がかさばらない略語が好んで使用されます

ルール：略語の場合でも、元々のアルファベットの文字の時と同じ読み方をする場合が多く見受けられます。（略語にはもってこいの）数字はそのままの読み方で使われます。しかし、中には略語として使われる先頭文字が元のアルファベットとまったく違った文字になることもあります。（例：CU = See you.）

1　Practice 1

1～5のそれぞれの略語について、下の四角の中から適切な意味の語句を選んで記入しなさい。

> **as soon as possible / at / great / later / see you / to / too / two**

1. GR8 = _____
2. @   = _____
3. ASAP = _____
4. 2   = _____
5. CU   = _____
6. L8R = _____

2　Practice 2

下の4つのそれぞれの文について、上で練習した略語（や短縮形）を使って表現してみましょう。（太字が略語で表現可能な箇所です。）

1. **Great**, we're **at** Java Hut　= _____
2. Come **as soon as possible**　= _____
3. I **want to** introduce **you to**~　= _____
4. **See you later**　= _____

3　Practice 3　[CD 2–8/DL 97]

下の文を読み、Practice 1 の 1〜6 の略語の中から適切なものを選び、空欄を埋めましょう。音声を聞いて答えをチェックしてみましょう。

Example: Let me know what you're doing L8R.

1. I have something important to tell you so come _____.
2. You got 100% on the test? That's _____!
3. Bye, _____.

上で学習した発音を特に意識して、50頁の会話をペアの相手と練習してみましょう。

SPEAKING   [Getting to know people]

私たちは毎日のように人と知り合いますが、人と接するのが上手な人でさえ、次に何を話したらよいのか戸惑うことがありますね。でも話題についてのリストを用意しておけば慌てることもありません。

1 Practice 1

まず、相手にしてみたい質問を下の空欄に記入します。次に3~4人のグループを作ります。普段話す機会の少ないクラスメートの方がいいでしょう。
順番に交代しながら、自分が書いた質問を相手にしてみましょう。

My questions:

1. _____
2. _____
3. _____
4. _____

2 Practice 2

下の表の左の欄に、グループの人たちの名前を書きます。その右の余白には、それぞれの人たちについて聞いた情報を記入していきましょう。

Name:	
Name:	
Name:	
Name:	

PROVERBS AND SAYINGS

1 Practice 1 [CD 2-9/DL 98]

英語のことわざ（名言）を（必要に応じて）数回聴いて書き取ります。次にグループになって書き取ったものを比べてみます。もう一度音声を聴いて、必要があれば訂正しながらグループの答えを書きましょう。最終的に全員が正答にたどり着けるようにしましょう。

1. _____ (9 words)

2 Practice 2

グループ内でこのことわざ（名言）の意味について話し合ってa～cの中から正解を選びましょう。

A. Be good and honest to all people but do not trust everyone.
B. Loving, trusting and doing good to others are the important things in life.
C. People who do bad things to others should not be trusted.

Useful phrases　この表現を使って話し合ってみよう

What did you hear?	What did you write?
What word did you write before ____?	What word did you write after ____?
How do you spell ____?	Look at my answer. Is anything missing?
What does ___ mean in Japanese?	What does this saying mean?

Chapter 10　A BLIND DATE

(Relationships 2)

VOCABULARY PREVIEW

1　Pronunciation Practice　[CD 2-10/DL 99]

英語の単語や表現を聞いて口頭で繰り返してください。

2　Dictation　[CD 2-10/DL 99]

もう一度同じ単語や表現を聞き下の1~8番の空欄に記入しましょう。次にスペルが正しく書けているかどうか隣同士ペアになってチェックし合います。その際、下の囲み内の表現を使いながら英語で相談してみましょう。

> **Useful phrases**　この表現を使って話し合ってみよう
>
> What did you hear for number ~ ?　　How do you spell ~ ?
> I heard ~　　　　　　　　　　　　　I think it's spelled _ _ _ _ _

1. authentic　　　　　　(e)　　5. _____ ( )
2. _____ ( )　　6. _____ ( )
3. _____ ( )　　7. _____ ( )
4. _____ ( )　　8. _____ ( )

3　Definitions

3、4人のグループを作ります。上の8つの単語や表現の定義として最もふさわしいものを下から選び、上のカッコ内に記号を記入しましょう。辞書は使わずにグループ内で英語で話し合って答えを選びます。その際、下の囲み内の表現を使ってみましょう。

a. ready and wanting to do or try something
b. a date where two people who do not know each other meet
c. not sleepy at all; fully attentive
d. a signal that tells a person to do something
e. real, true and like the original
f. a dish from South America with raw fish, citrus juice and spices
g. to sleep for a short time, usually during the day
h. to put something in a liquid for a long time

> **Useful phrases**　この表現を使って話し合ってみよう
>
> Are you ready? I'll read the definition and you choose the best word.
> What is ~ ?　　　　　　　　　　　I'm not sure. Maybe it is ~
> I think so too.　　　　　OR　　　I agree.
> I disagree. I think the answer is ~ .

SHORT DIALOG

まず右の頁の質問文に目を通してから会話文 (Part 1) を読みましょう。次に会話を聴いてそれぞれの質問に答えます。会話文の後半 (Part 2) は印刷されていませんので集中して聴きましょう。

> *Situation*: Jack has arranged a blind date for Toshi. Toshi and his date are about to meet for the first time.

Part 1

[1] [CD 2–11/DL 100]

Toshi: Jack, I was wondering if you could tell me a little about Rosy before we meet for our blind date. In Japan people usually go out in a group when meeting for the first time.

Jack: Sure! As you know, I met her through Laura. She has brown hair and brown eyes and is fairly tall. She loves to go out dancing on the weekends and she works at her family's restaurant when she is not studying.

Toshi: What type of restaurant does her family own?

[2] [CD 2–12/DL 101]

Jack: Why don't you ask her yourself? Here she comes. I will stay to introduce the two of you but then I should leave so you can get to know each other. Rosy, hi! Let me introduce you to my friend, Toshi.

Rosy: Hi Toshi, how are you? Jack has told me a lot about you. I'm looking forward to having dinner with you tonight.

Jack: Well, I think that's my cue to leave. Have a great night and I hope the two of you enjoy dinner together.

[3] [CD 2–13/DL 102]

Toshi: Rosy, where would you like to eat? There's a great Italian restaurant around the corner.

Rosy: I was thinking I could bring you to my family's new restaurant. We are originally from Mexico and my father recently opened a restaurant here, in California.

Toshi: I normally don't eat too much spice and have never really tried authentic Mexican food but I am up for anything tonight!

The conversation continues in Part 2.

Notes

wonder「〜かしらと思う」／ **fairly**「かなり」／ **own**「所有する」／ **look forward to ~ing**「〜するのを楽しみに待つ」／ **authentic**「本物の、本格的な」

Question 1: What is Toshi doing tonight?

   A. He is going on a date with someone he has never met.
   B. He is going on a date with someone he met through Laura.
   C. He is going on a date with Jack, Laura and someone new.

Question 2: What does Jack mean when he says "… that's my cue to leave"?

   A. He has a date soon and has to go meet Laura.
   B. Someone is calling his phone and wants to answer it.
   C. He has been there long enough, now it is time to go.

Question 3: Why does Toshi say "I'm up for anything tonight"?

   A. He finished studying and has free time.
   B. He just had a nap and feels wide-awake.
   C. He is willing to try new things tonight.

Part 2 [CD 2-14~16/DL 103~105]

(*Toshi and Rosy go to her family's Mexican restaurant and now they have finished eating. They are making plans.*)

Question 4: Toshi would like to see Rosy again.

   T   F

Question 5: Rosy does not want to try sushi.

   T   F

Question 6: Toshi and Rosy will go on another blind date.

   T   F

Notes

   ceviche「セビチェ」南米料理。魚介類に玉ねぎや香辛料、レモン汁などの材料を使って作る。

PRONUNCIATION　ポイント：通信 (SNS) 用の略語を使った簡潔な表現その２

現代の若者の間では、メールやチャットで親しい友人などとメッセージをやり取りする時は、文字数がかさばらない略語が好んで使用されます

ルール：略語の場合でも、元々のアルファベットの文字の時と同じ読み方をする場合が多く見受けられます。（略語にはもってこいの）数字はそのままの読み方で使われます。しかし、中には略語として使われる先頭文字が元のアルファベットとまったく違った文字になることもあります。（例：CU = See you. GF= Girlfriend. BF =Boyfriend. BBS= Be back soon.）

1　Practice 1

1~10 のそれぞれの略語について、下の四角の中から適切な意味の語句を選んで記入しなさい。

> bye for now,　forward,　goodbye,　good idea,　good to see you,
> meet me at,　message,　message me back,　tonight

1. BTW: by the way
2. BFN: _____
3. 2NITE: _____
4. FWD: _____
5. GB: _____
6. GI: _____
7. MMA: _____
8. MSG: _____
9. MMB: _____
10. GTCU: _____

2　Practice 2　[CD 2–17/DL 106]

下の略語が含まれたメッセージを読んで、通常の英文に書き直してみましょう。その際、上の練習で学んだ表現をぜひ応用してみましょう。完成したら、音声を聴いて（もしくは先生と一緒に）答えをチェックしましょう。

(*Example*: GTCU last night. = Good to see you last night)

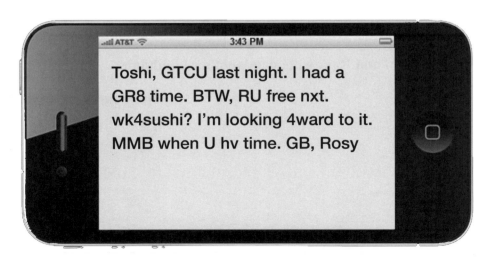

Toshi, GTCU last night. I had a GR8 time. BTW, RU free nxt. wk4sushi? I'm looking 4ward to it. MMB when U hv time. GB, Rosy

Answer: _____

_____
_____
_____
_____
_____
_____

SPEAKING [A response to Rosy's text message from Toshi]

1 Practice 1

58頁のRosyのメッセージに対する返信を書きます。まず、ペアを組んで二人で一緒にRosyからToshiへのメッセージをもう一度よく読み直してみましょう。次に、二人で相談しながら自分たちがToshiになったつもりで、Rosyへの適切な返信を書いてみましょう。その際、先ほど学んだ略語を大いに活用して下さい。

_____
_____
_____
_____
_____
_____
_____
_____
_____
_____

2 Practice 2

Rosyに伝わるメッセージができましたか。書き終わったら、隣のペアにあなた方の作った返信文を声に出して読んでもらいましょう。読む時は58頁を見ずに読みます。略語の読み方はもう覚えましたね。

PROVERBS AND SAYINGS

1 **Practice 1** [CD 2-18/DL 107]

英語のことわざ（名言）を（必要に応じて）数回聴いて書き取ります。次にグループになって書き取ったものを比べてみます。もう一度音声を聴いて、必要があれば訂正しながらグループの答えを書きましょう。最終的に全員が正答にたどり着けるようにしましょう。

1. _____ (10 words)

2 **Practice 2**

グループ内でこのことわざ（名言）の意味について話し合ってa～cの中から正解を選びましょう。

a. If you want to live a good life you need family.
b. If you give to others your life will be complete.
c. If you live with many people you cannot focus on work.

Useful phrases　この表現を使って話し合ってみよう

What did you hear?	What did you write?
What word did you write before ____?	What word did you write after ____?
How do you spell _____?	Look at my answer. Is anything missing?
What does ___ mean in Japanese?	What does this saying mean?

Chapter 11　APPLYING FOR WORK
(Work 1)

VOCABULARY PREVIEW

1 Pronunciation Practice [CD 2-19/DL 108]

英語の単語や表現を聞いて口頭で繰り返してください。

2 Dictation [CD 2-19/DL 108]

もう一度同じ単語や表現を聞き下の1~8番の空欄に記入しましょう。次にスペルが正しく書けているかどうか隣同士ペアになってチェックし合います。その際、下の囲み内の表現を使いながら英語で相談してみましょう。

> **Useful phrases**　この表現を使って話し合ってみよう
>
> What did you hear for number ~ ?　　How do you spell ~ ?
> I heard ~　　　　　　　　　　　　　I think it's spelled _ _ _ _ _

1. __allow_____ (f)　　5. _____ (　)
2. _____ (　)　　6. _____ (　)
3. _____ (　)　　7. _____ (　)
4. _____ (　)　　8. _____ (　)

3 Definitions

3、4人のグループを作ります。上の8つの単語や表現の定義として最もふさわしいものを下から選び、上のカッコ内に記号を記入しましょう。辞書は使わずにグループ内で英語で話し合って答えを選びます。その際、下の囲み内の表現を使ってみましょう。

a. to talk or write about something or someone in a brief way
b. the period of time in the year when a university has classes
c. a document used to make a formal request for something
d. words on a sign showing a shop is looking for new workers
e. to make a positive comment about someone
f. to permit; to let someone have or do something
g. demanding that people follow the rules or act a certain way
h. something you cannot do by law or the rules of a game

> **Useful phrases**　この表現を使って話し合ってみよう
>
> Are you ready? I'll read the definition and you choose the best word.
> What is ~ ?　　　　　　　　　　　I'm not sure. Maybe it is ~
> I think so too.　　　　　　OR　　　I agree.
> I disagree. I think the answer is ~ .

SHORT DIALOG

まず右の頁の質問文に目を通してから会話文 (Part 1) を読みましょう。次に会話を聴いてそれぞれの質問に答えます。会話文の後半 (Part 2) は印刷されていませんので集中して聴きましょう。

Situation: Toshi meets Jack on campus. He's thinking about applying for a job at the campus bookstore and wants Jack to help him.

Part 1

[1] [CD 2–20/DL 109]

Toshi: I'm thinking about getting a part-time job. I saw a "help wanted" sign in the window at the university bookstore so I went in and got an application.

Jack: That sounds really great Toshi, but why **don't you** get a job at the Java Hut? We're always looking for people to work part-time.

Toshi: Because of my student visa rules I'm not allowed to work off-campus.

[2] [CD 2–21/DL 110]

Jack: I didn't know that? Why not?

Toshi: If I stayed here **next year** I could work off campus but **first year** international students are only allowed to work up to 20 hours a week at a job on-campus while classes are in session. It's illegal for me to get a job off-campus.

Jack: Wow! I had no idea that the rules were so strict for international students.

[3] [CD 2–22/DL 111]

Toshi: Yes, Mr. Price helped me with so many things **last year** before I left Japan. He explained lots of rules and he helped me write my application letter in English. He also taught me about American culture.

Jack: Who is Mr. Price? I've never heard you mention him.

Toshi: He is the student advisor at my university's International Exchange Center. He is so helpful to all the exchange students.

The conversation continues in Part 2.

Notes

application「応募、申込（用紙）」

Question 1: Why doesn't Toshi apply to work at the Java Hut with Jack?

A. He doesn't think his English is good enough yet.
B. Toshi is not looking for work at a coffee shop.
C. Toshi can only work at a job that is on-campus.

Question 2: How many hours a week is Toshi allowed to work part-time?

A. He can work fewer than 19.5 hours.
B. He can work up to 20 hours.
C. He can work more than 20 hours

Question 3: How did Mr. Price help international exchange students?

A. He wrote their letters and taught them American culture.
B. He helped them to write letters and he made rules to follow.
C. He explained rules and helped them to complete forms.

Part 2 [CD 2-23~25/DL 112~114]

Question 4: Jack will say good things about Toshi to his friend.

    T   F

Question 5: Toshi wants Jack to complete the job application for him.

    T   F

Question 6: Toshi will buy pizza for dinner to thank Jack for helping him.

    T   F

Notes

apply to ~「～に応募する」/ **put in a good word for ~**「～のために口添えする、推薦する」/ **fill out**「書き込む、記入する」

PRONUNCIATION　ポイント：音同士が同化して生まれる「ch」の音 ②

> ルール：下のような語句を自然な速さで発音するとき、単語の末尾の「t」の音が、後ろに続く単語の冒頭の「y（発音 :/juː/）」とつながり同化することで、「ch（発音 :/tʃ/）」の音が生まれます。

1　Practice 1　[CD 2-26/DL 115]

音声の後に続けて発音してみましょう。

Meet you	Meechu
Don't you	Donchu
Want you	Wanchu
Last year	Laschear

2　Practice 2　[CD 2-27/DL 116]

音声を聞いて、下の例文を練習しましょう。まず、通常の発音での文が流れます。次に、音同士がつながった形の文が流れます。ペアの相手と両方の形の例文を発音してみましょう。

Why **don't you** get a job?	Why *donchu* get a job?
I'm in my **first year** of studies.	I'm in my *firschear* of studies.
He helped me a lot **last year**.	He helped me a lot *laschear*.

3　Practice 3　[CD 2-28/DL 117]

下の文を読み、上の例文の太字の語句の中から適切なものを選び、空欄を埋めましょう。音声を聞いて答えをチェックしてみましょう。

Example: I've heard so many good things about you.

1. I ＿＿＿＿＿＿＿＿＿＿＿＿ to complete page 39 in your textbook for homework.

2. Why ＿＿＿＿＿＿＿＿＿＿＿＿ like sushi?

3. I have wanted to ＿＿＿＿＿＿＿＿＿＿＿＿ for so long.

上で学習した発音を特に意識して、62頁の会話をペアの相手と練習してみましょう。

SPEAKING [Job application]

1 Practice 1

下の、仕事の応募用紙を読んでみましょう。3~4人のグループになって、不明な単語があれば話し合いながら、自分の詳細を書き入れてみましょう。辞書を使ってもかまいません。実際に応募する状況にある自分を想像して、出来るだけ空欄を埋めてみましょう。

UNIVERSITY BOOKSTORE APPLICATION FORM

The bookstore is divided into several departments. Check below the department in which your work experience or personal interest would be best suited.

____ Cards and gifts   ____ Cashier   ____ Clothing   ____ Book Sales   ____ Stocking

How many hours can you work each week? Minimum: _____ Maximum: _____

When can you begin to work? _____

Name: _____   Phone number: _____

Local address: _____

Email: _____   Major: _____

Please list information from your previous employer

Employer: _____   Phone number: _____

Type of business: _____   Job title: _____

Employed from: _____ to _____   Supervisor: _____

Please answer the following questions:

Why are you interested in working for the university bookstore? _____
_____

List specific work knowledge or experience that is connected to the position you desire: _____
_____
_____

PROVERBS AND SAYINGS

1 Practice 1 [CD 2-29/DL 118]

英語のことわざ（名言）を（必要に応じて）数回聴いて書き取ります。次にグループになって書き取ったものを比べてみます。もう一度音声を聴いて、必要があれば訂正しながらグループの答えを書きましょう。最終的に全員が正答にたどり着けるようにしましょう。

1. _____

   _____ (11 words)

2 Practice 2

グループ内でこのことわざ（名言）の意味について話し合ってa〜cの中から正解を選びましょう。

a. To be successful at work you must study vocabulary.
b. Using a dictionary is the best way to learn to spell words.
c. You must work really hard before you can be successful.

Useful phrases　この表現を使って話し合ってみよう

What did you hear?	What did you write?
What word did you write before ____?	What word did you write after ____?
How do you spell _____?	Look at my answer. Is anything missing?
What does ___ mean in Japanese?	What does this saying mean?

Chapter 12 A JOB INTERVIEW
(Work 2)

VOCABULARY PREVIEW

1 Pronunciation Practice [CD 2-30/DL 119]
英語の単語や表現を聞いて口頭で繰り返してください。

2 Dictation [CD 2-30/DL 119]
もう一度同じ単語や表現を聞き下の1~8番の空欄に記入しましょう。次にスペルが正しく書けているかどうか隣同士ペアになってチェックし合います。その際、下の囲み内の表現を使いながら英語で相談してみましょう。

> **Useful phrases**　この表現を使って話し合ってみよう
>
> What did you hear for number ~ ?　　How do you spell ~ ?
> I heard ~　　　　　　　　　　　　　I think it's spelled _ _ _ _ _

1. available (f)　　5. _____ ( )
2. _____ ( )　　6. _____ ( )
3. _____ ( )　　7. _____ ( )
4. _____ ( )　　8. _____ ( )

3 Definitions
3、4人のグループを作ります。上の8つの単語や表現の定義として最もふさわしいものを下から選び、上のカッコ内に記号を記入しましょう。辞書を使わずにグループ内で英語で話し合って答えを選びます。その際、下の囲み内の表現を使ってみましょう。

a. deserving respect or attention; making a good impression
b. to think about something carefully so you can make a decision
c. to enter someone as a member or a participant in something
d. a job
e. a short document showing your work and education history
f. something that is possible to get
g. having the skill, experience or knowledge needed to do a job
h. the way you treat someone, especially used with customers

> **Useful phrases**　この表現を使って話し合ってみよう
>
> Are you ready? I'll read the definition and you choose the best word.
> What is ~ ?　　　　　　　　　　　I'm not sure. Maybe it is ~
> I think so too.　　　　　OR　　　I agree.
> I disagree. I think the answer is ~ .

SHORT DIALOG

まず右の頁の質問文に目を通してから会話文 (Part 1) を読みましょう。次に会話を聴いてそれぞれの質問に答えます。会話文の後半 (Part 2) は印刷されていませんので集中して聴きましょう。

Situation: Toshi sent his application to the university bookstore. He is getting ready to begin the interview with the manager.

Part 1

[1] [CD 2–31/DL 120]

Manager: Hello Toshi. It's nice to meet you. My name is Tony Jones and I'm the manager at the university bookstore. I'll be interviewing you today about the job opening **that's available**.

Toshi: It's nice to meet you Mr. Jones. **Thank you** for considering my application.

Manager: Well, you seem pretty qualified from your résumé. I'd like to **ask you** a few questions first and then **if you** have any questions you **can ask** me after I'm done.

[2] [CD 2–32/DL 121]

Toshi: OK, that sounds good. To tell you the truth, I'm a bit nervous. This is my first job interview in English.

Manager: Just relax Toshi. Do your best to answer my questions. First, what is your major and do you have any experience in sales?

Toshi: I'm a business major at my university in Tokyo. For the first semester here in Los Angeles I'm taking mostly general English courses. I plan on enrolling in some business courses next semester.

[3] [CD 2–33/DL 122]

Manager: OK, and do you have any special skills connected to this position? I'm sure you know that our college bookstore doesn't just sell books!

Toshi: Yes, I have had part-time jobs working in restaurants in Tokyo. I'm really good at dealing with customers. I have also worked in an Internet café. We provide many different services for customers and there are always books there for people to read.

Manager: Well that sounds impressive Toshi. Do you have any questions you'd like to ask me?

The conversation continues in Part 2.

Notes

job opening「欠員、募集中のポスト」/ **consider**「検討する」/ **résumé**「履歴書」/ **sales**「販売、営業」/ **enroll**「（授業やコースに）登録する」/ **skill**「技能、スキル」/ **deal with~**「～に応対する、対処する」

68　SOUNDS REAL!

Question 1: What is the managers opinion of Toshi's resume?

  A. Toshi's resume seems incomplete.
  B. Toshi's resume looks very pretty.
  C. Toshi's experience seems suitable.

Question 2: What is Toshi studying at university this semester?

  A. He's studying general English courses.
  B. He's studying business courses.
  C. He's studying general education courses.

Question 3: Where has Toshi worked in the past?

  A. In a restaurant and in a bookstore.
  B. In a restaurant and in an Internet café.
  C. In an Internet café and in a bookstore.

Part 2 [CD 2-34~36/DL 123~125]

Question 4: The bookstore only needs students to work on-campus.

　　　T　　F

Question 5: The manager offers Toshi a job at the bookstore.

　　　T　　F

Question 6: Toshi starts working on Monday.

　　　T　　F

Notes
  get into trouble「トラブルになる、面倒なことに巻き込まれる」

PRONUNCIATION　ポイント：末尾の音と冒頭の音がつながり同化する音

ルール：英語の発音での最も典型的な音の同化の形の一つとして、末尾が子音の音で終わる単語に、冒頭が母音（a e i o u）で始まる単語がつながるケースがあります。

1 Practice 1 [CD 2-37/DL 126]

音声の後に続けて発音してみましょう。

Thank you	= Thankyu
If you	= Iffyu
Ask you	= Askyu
Can ask	= Canask

2 Practice 2 [CD 2-38/DL 127]

音声を聞いて、下の例文を練習しましょう。まず、通常の発音での文が流れます。次に、音同士がつながった形の文が流れます。ペアの相手と両方の形の例文を発音してみましょう。

Thank you for considering my application.　　　*Thankyu* for…
I'd like to **ask you** a few questions　　　I'd like to *askyu*…
If you have any questions you **can ask** me after.　　　*Iffyu* have any…
　　　　　　　　　　　　　　　　　　　　　　　　　you *canask* me…

3 Practice 3 [CD 2-39/DL 128]

下の文を読み、上の例文の太字の語句の中から適切なものを選び、空欄を埋めましょう。
音声を聞いて答えをチェックしてみましょう。

Example: I'll be interviewing you for the job that's available.

1. I _____ Mr. Price to help me write my letter.

2. Joshua wants to _____ out on a date.

3. _____ don't like it, don't eat it.

上で学習した発音を特に意識して、68 頁の会話をペアの相手と練習してみましょう。

SPEAKING [Adjectives to describe people]

1 Practice 1

ペアになって囲み内の表現を使って相談しながら、下の1～25の形容詞の意味（日本語）を記入していきましょう。いくつ分かりましたか。二人とも分からない単語は辞書を使って調べましょう。

Adjectives to describe people

1. aggressive (　　　)
2. ambitious (　　　)
3. beautiful (　　　)
4. careful (　　　)
5. chatty (　　　)
6. competitive (　　　)
7. confident (　　　)
8. considerate (　　　)
9. courageous (　　　)
10. creative (　　　)
11. energetic (　　　)
12. fashionable (　　　)
13. handsome (　　　)
14. hard-working (　　　)
15. helpful (　　　)
16. honest (　　　)
17. intelligent (　　　)
18. kind (　　　)
19. lazy (　　　)
20. outgoing (　　　)
21. patient (　　　)
22. punctual (　　　)
23. reliable (　　　)
24. sensitive (　　　)
25. strong (　　　)

Useful Expressions　この表現を使って話し合ってみよう

What does (patient) mean?
I don't know, let's look it up in the dictionary.
It means (がまん強い) in Japanese.　OR　It means a person who (can wait a long time).

---

2 Practice 2

今度は、3~4人のグループになります。72頁の職種一覧リストを見て、それぞれどんな職業かを確認し合います。次に、それぞれの職業にふさわしい適性を表している形容詞を上のリストから少なくとも3つ選び出して、表に書き入れていきましょう。その際、下の表現を使って話し合います。余力があるグループは、空欄にさらにこれ以外の職業とその適性を表す形容詞を書いてみましょう。出来るだけたくさんの形容詞を使ってみましょう。

Useful Expressions　この表現を使って話し合ってみよう

What characteristics should a _____ have?
What kind of person should a _____ be?
A _____ should be _____, _____, and _____ because _____.

Occupation	List adjectives from the Practice 1 or use your own
Lawyer	
Firefighter	
Police officer	
Nurse	
Pro athlete	
Homemaker	
Business Manager	
Fashion Model	

PROVERBS AND SAYINGS

1 Practice 1 [CD 2–40/DL 129]

英語のことわざ（名言）を（必要に応じて）数回聴いて書き取ります。次にグループになって書き取ったものを比べてみます。もう一度音声を聴いて、必要があれば訂正しながらグループの答えを書きましょう。最終的に全員が正答にたどり着けるようにしましょう。

1. _____ (8 words)

2 Practice 2

グループ内でこのことわざ（名言）の意味について話し合って
a～cの中から正解を選びましょう。

a. If you don't work hard you'll stay good looking but will not be happy.
b. Although relaxing seems enjoyable, hard work makes you feel good.
c. Attractive people don't have to work very hard to be satisfied.

Useful phrases　この表現を使って話し合ってみよう

What did you hear?　　　　　　　　　　What did you write?
What word did you write before ____?　What word did you write after____?
How do you spell _____?　　　　　　　Look at my answer. Is anything missing?
What does ___ mean in Japanese?　　　What does this saying mean?

Chapter 13 SPANISH LESSONS

(Future plans 1)

VOCABULARY PREVIEW

1 Pronunciation Practice [CD 2–41/DL 130]

英語の単語や表現を聞いて口頭で繰り返してください。

2 Dictation [CD 2–41/DL 130]

もう一度同じ単語や表現を聞き下の 1~8 番の空欄に記入しましょう。次にスペルが正しく書けているかどうか隣同士ペアになってチェックし合います。その際、下の囲み内の表現を使いながら英語で相談してみましょう。

> **Useful phrases**　この表現を使って話し合ってみよう
>
> What did you hear for number ~ ?　　How do you spell ~ ?
> I heard ~　　　　　　　　　　　　　I think it's spelled _ _ _ _ _

1. __canned goods_____ (f)　　5. _____ ( )
2. _____ ( )　　6. _____ ( )
3. _____ ( )　　7. _____ ( )
4. _____ ( )　　8. _____ ( )

3 Definitions

3、4人のグループを作ります。上の 8 つの単語や表現の定義として最もふさわしいものを下から選び、上のカッコ内に記号を記入しましょう。辞書は使わずにグループ内で英語で話し合って答えを選びます。その際、下の囲み内の表現を使ってみましょう。

a. liking to be with and talk to other people
b. to give something to help a person or a group
c. very good at thinking or learning about things
d. a group or center that collects food and gives it to the needy
e. to make progress or to do well in order to be successful
f. food that has been put in a can and can stay fresh a long time
g. having a kind and loving character
h. connected to Spanish speaking people or culture

> **Useful phrases**　この表現を使って話し合ってみよう
>
> Are you ready? I'll read the definition and you choose the best word.
> What is ~ ?　　　　　　　　　　　I'm not sure. Maybe it is ~
> I think so too.　　　　　　OR　　　I agree.
> I disagree. I think the answer is ~ .

SHORT DIALOG

まず右の頁の質問文に目を通してから会話文 (Part 1) を読みましょう。次に会話を聴いてそれぞれの質問に答えます。会話文の後半 (Part 2) は印刷されていませんので集中して聴きましょう。

> ***Situation***: Toshi talks to Jack about his date with Rosy. He has decided that he wants to start studying Spanish.

Part 1

[1] [CD 2–42/DL 131]

Toshi: Jack, thank you so much for introducing me to Rosy. I had a fantastic time. We've already arranged for a second date, too! We're going to go out for sushi.

Jack: That's great to hear Toshi. She is one of Laura's best friends so I thought you'd **like her**. She's warm and outgoing, and she's also very serious and smart.

Toshi: I really enjoyed the Mexican food we ate; her dad is a great cook. You know Jack, I'm thinking about studying Spanish, but don't **tell her** that.

[2] [CD 2–43/DL 132]

Jack: Wow! You two really must have hit it off! As a matter of fact, I study Spanish at the community center Sunday afternoons. Why don't you come with me next time?

Toshi: But you must be advanced. I'm just a beginner.

Jack: No problem Toshi, you have to start somewhere. There are different classes according to ability.

[3] [CD 2–44/DL 133]

Toshi: Well I guess it's worth a try. How much do the lessons cost?

Jack: The teachers are volunteers so classes are free. Bring some canned goods to donate to the local food bank if you want though.

Toshi: By the way Jack, Laura is not from Mexico so why do you study Spanish?

The conversation continues in Part 2.

Notes

arrange「準備・手配する、話を取り決める」/ **hit it off**「意気投合する、ウマが合う」/ **advanced**「上級（レベル）の」/ **according to~**「~に従って、~に応じて」/ **donate**「寄付する」

Question 1: What does Jack say about Rosy?

    A. Many people like her.
    B. She likes to meet new people.
    C. She likes to keep in shape.

Question 2: Where does Jack study Spanish?

    A. At the community center.
    B. He studies somewhere.
    C. In a beginner's class.

Question 3: Why are the lessons free of charge?

    A. Because teachers volunteer their time to teach Spanish.
    B. Because the Community Center can get canned goods.
    C. Because students volunteer to learn.

Part 2 [CD 2–45~47/DL 134~136]

Question 4: About 40% of all Americans speak Spanish.

    T   F

Question 5: Jack has two part-time jobs.

    T   F

Question 6: Jack will surprise Rosy with the news.

    T   F

Notes
    huge「巨大な、大規模な」/ **benefit**「利益、恩恵」/ **get ahead**「出世する」/ **sure thing**「もちろん」

PRONUNCIATION　ポイント：「h」の音の脱落による音のつながり

> ルール：自然な速さでの発音の場合「his」「him」「her」といった単語が子音の後に続いて発音されるとき、「h」の音にはアクセントが置かれないため、発音されずに、単語同士がなめらかにつながります。

1　Practice 1　[CD 2–48/DL 137]

音声の後に続けて発音してみましょう。

Like her	= Liker
Tell her	= Teller
Send him	= Sendim
Let her	= Letter

2　Practice 2　[CD 2–49/DL 138]

音声を聞いて、下の例文を練習しましょう。まず、通常の発音での文が流れます。次に、音同士がつながった形の文が流れます。ペアの相手と両方の形の例文を発音してみましょう。

I thought you'd **like her**.	I thought you'd *liker*.
I won't **let her** know.	I won't *letter* know.
I want to **surprise her**.	I want to *surpriser*.

3　Practice 3　[CD 2–50/DL 139]

下の文を読み、上の例文の太字の語句の中から適切なものを選び、空欄を埋めましょう。音声を聞いて答えをチェックしてみましょう。

Example: Don't <u>tell her</u> about the surprise party.

1. Do you want to _____ with the news?

2. If you really _____ you should tell her.

3. Could you please _____ know that I called?

上で学習した発音を特に意識して、74頁の会話をペアの相手と練習してみましょう。

SPEAKING [Continuing a conversation]

1 Practice 1

まず下の表の左列の YES / NO 形式の質問をペアの相手といっしょに読んでいきます。次に、右列のさらに詳しく尋ねるフォローアップ質問を協力して完成させます。それが完成したら、今度はお互い新しい相手とペアになり、YES / NO 質問を尋ねます。相手の答えが YES であれば、続けてフォローアップ質問をします。相手の答えは表の下の解答欄に記入していきましょう

Example: Are you going to go out this weekend? Who are you going with?

	YES / NO Style Questions	Follow-up question
	Are you going to…	
1	…travel after you graduate?	Where would you _____?
2	…save some money?	Why _____?
3	…learn something new?	What _____?
4	…have a big family?	How many people _____?
5	…start looking for a job?	When _____?

Answer

1. _____
2. _____
3. _____
4. _____
5. _____

Chapter 13 SPANISH LESSONS (Future plans 1)

PROVERBS AND SAYINGS

1 Practice 1 [CD 2–51/DL 140]

英語のことわざ（名言）を（必要に応じて）数回聴いて書き取ります。次にグループになって書き取ったものを比べてみます。もう一度音声を聴いて、必要があれば訂正しながらグループの答えを書きましょう。最終的に全員が正答にたどり着けるようにしましょう。

1. _____ (9 words)

2 Practice 2

グループ内でこのことわざ（名言）の意味について話し合って a～c の中から正解を選びましょう。

a. Many people wish for their goals to come true.
b. For a goal to become a reality we must take action.
c. Good planning is more important than wishing.

Useful phrases　この表現を使って話し合ってみよう

What did you hear?	What did you write?
What word did you write before ____?	What word did you write after ____?
How do you spell _____?	Look at my answer. Is anything missing?
What does ___ mean in Japanese?	What does this saying mean?

78　SOUNDS REAL!

Chapter 14 SPRING BREAK

(Future plans 2)

VOCABULARY PREVIEW

1 Pronunciation Practice [CD 2-52/DL 141]

英語の単語や表現を聞いて口頭で繰り返してください。

2 Dictation [CD 2-52/DL 141]

もう一度同じ単語や表現を聞き下の 1~8 番の空欄に記入しましょう。次にスペルが正しく書けているかどうか隣同士ペアになってチェックし合います。その際、下の囲み内の表現を使いながら英語で相談してみましょう。

> **Useful phrases**　この表現を使って話し合ってみよう
>
> What did you hear for number ~ ?　　How do you spell ~ ?
> I heard ~　　　　　　　　　　　　　I think it's spelled _ _ _ _ _

1. __definite_____ (g)　　5. _____ (   )
2. _____ (   )　　6. _____ (   )
3. _____ (   )　　7. _____ (   )
4. _____ (   )　　8. _____ (   )

3 Definitions

3、4 人のグループを作ります。上の 8 つの単語や表現の定義として最もふさわしいものを下から選び、上のカッコ内に記号を記入しましょう。辞書は使わずにグループ内で英語で話し合って答えを選びます。その際、下の囲み内の表現を使ってみましょう。

a. a person who is invited to stay in someone's home
b. during the time before something happens
c. a chance to do something
d. to think about problems or fears
e. listen to and understand what I'm saying
f. time for rest or recreation away from usual work or study
g. something that is already set or decided
h. something that is not correct

> **Useful phrases**　この表現を使って話し合ってみよう
>
> Are you ready? I'll read the definition and you choose the best word.
> What is ~ ?　　　　　　　　　　I'm not sure. Maybe it is ~
> I think so too.　　　　　OR　　I agree.
> I disagree. I think the answer is ~ .

SHORT DIALOG

まず右の頁の質問文に目を通してから会話文 (Part 1) を読みましょう。次に会話を聴いてそれぞれの質問に答えます。会話文の後半 (Part 2) は印刷されていませんので集中して聴きましょう。

> *Situation*: Jack and Laura will travel to Mexico with Rosy for Spring Break. Jack is asking Toshi if he can join them on their trip.

Part 1

[1] [CD 2–53/DL 142]

Jack: What are you **planning** to do for Spring Break Toshi?

Toshi: I don't have anything planned yet. I have to check my work schedule at the bookstore.

Jack: I think the bookstore is closed during Spring Break. Anyhow Toshi, Spring Break is not for **working** or **studying**, it's a time to have fun! Come to Mexico!

[2] [CD 2–54/DL 143]

Toshi: Well, if I have time off from work and I can enter Mexico on my student visa then I'd love to go with you. Who are you **going** with?

Jack: Laura and I are **going** and – get this – so is Rosy! She'll be visiting her family.

Toshi: What?! You want me to go on a trip with Rosy?

[3] [CD 2–55/DL 144]

Jack: Toshi, this is the perfect opportunity to practice your Spanish and to show Rosy how hard you have been **studying** since you started your lessons at the Community Center.

Toshi: But I can't speak Spanish well. What if I make a fool of myself?

Jack: The best way to learn something is by **doing** it. We learn by **making** mistakes.

The conversation continues in Part 2.

Notes

make a fool of oneself「ばかを見る、笑いものになる」

Question 1: What will Toshi do for Spring Break?

A. He'll work part-time at the bookstore.
B. He hasn't made any definite plans yet.
C. He'll study for his exams.

Question 2: So far, who is going to Mexico?

A. Jack, Laura and Rosy.
B. Jack and Laura.
C. Rosy and her family.

Question 3: Why is this trip a great opportunity for Toshi?

A. He will be able to practice Spanish in Mexico.
B. He will be able to show Rosy around Mexico.
C. He will have the chance to make mistakes.

Part 2 [CD 2-56~58/DL 145~147]

Question 4: Jack, Laura and Toshi can stay with Rosy's family.

  T F

Question 5: Jack, Laura, Toshi and Rosy will meet to discuss the trip.

  T F

Question 6: Jack tells Toshi to start organizing for the trip.

  T F

Chichen Itza

Notes
 detail「詳細」／ **in the meantime**「それまでは、さしあたり」

PRONUNCIATION　ポイント：「~ing 形」の「g」の音が脱落した発音

> ルール：「~ing 形」の動詞をはじめ、末尾が「~ing」となる単語はすべて「~ing」と発音される代わりに、しばしば「~in」と発音されます。

1　Practice 1　[CD 2-59/DL 148]

音声の後に続けて発音してみましょう。

Planning	= Plannin'
Working	= Workin'
Studying	= Studyin'
Going	= Goin'

2　Practice 2　[CD 2-60/DL 149]

音声を聞いて、下の例文を練習しましょう。まず、通常の発音での文が流れます。次に、音同士がつながった形の文が流れます。ペアの相手と両方の形の例文を発音してみましょう。

We learn by **making** mistakes.　　　We learn by *makin'* mistakes.
Who are you **going** with?　　　Who are you *goin'* with?
We'll be **staying** with her family.　　　We'll be *stayin'* with her family.

3　Practice 3　[CD 2-61/DL 150]

下の文を読み、上の例文の太字の語句の中から適切なものを選び、空欄を埋めましょう。音声を聞いて答えをチェックしてみましょう。

Example: The best way to learn something is by <u>doing</u> it.

1. Who is _____ to the party after the orientation session?

2. Stop _____ so much noise and listen to the announcement.

3. I have a big test tomorrow so I'm _____ home tonight to study.

上で学習した発音を特に意識して、80頁の会話をペアの相手と練習してみましょう。

SPEAKING [Describing things you like and dislike doing]

1 Practice 1

自分の好きなことや嫌いなことを、下の5つの文の空所を埋めながら書いていきましょう。完成したら、今度はペアを組んだ相手の同様の情報を聞いて、もう一つの5つの文の空所を完成させていきましょう。その際、下の質問表現を使って相手の好きなことや嫌いなことを聞いてみましょう。

My information

1. I love _____ing _____
2. I enjoy _____ing _____
3. I don't mind _____ing _____
4. I don't like _____ing _____
5. I can't stand _____ing _____

Tell me about yourself.   What things do you like and not like doing?

My partner's information

1. _____ loves _____ing _____
2. _____ enjoys _____ing _____
3. _____ doesn't mind _____ing _____
4. _____ doesn't like _____ing _____
5. _____ can't stand _____ing _____

Useful phrases

going camping / studying English / playing video games / hiking in the mountains
going to hot springs / reading books / listening to music

Chapter 14 SPRING BREAK (Future plans 2)

PROVERBS AND SAYINGS

1 Practice 1 [CD 2–62/DL 151]

英語のことわざ（名言）を（必要に応じて）数回聴いて書き取ります。次にグループになって書き取ったものを比べてみます。もう一度音声を聴いて、必要があれば訂正しながらグループの答えを書きましょう。最終的に全員が正答にたどり着けるようにしましょう。

1. _____

_____ (12 words)

2 Practice 2

グループ内でこのことわざ（名言）の意味についてa～cの中から正解を選びましょう。

a. It's important to keep your house in good condition.
b. It's best to get your work done during daylight hours.
c. Don't wait until it is too late to do what needs doing.

> **Useful phrases**　この表現を使って話し合ってみよう
>
> What did you hear?　　　　　　　　　What did you write?
> What word did you write before ____?　What word did you write after____?
> How do you spell _____?　　　　　　Look at my answer. Is anything missing?
> What does ___ mean in Japanese?　　What does this saying mean?

Chapter 15 REVIEW

VOCABULARY REVIEW

1 Pronunciation Practice [CD 2-63~65/DL 152~154]

英語の単語や表現を聞いて口頭で繰り返してください。

2 Dictation [CD 2-63~65/DL 152~154]

もう一度同じ単語や表現を聞き下の1~15番の空欄左側に記入しましょう。次にスペルが正しく書けているかどうか隣同士ペアになってチェックし合います。その際、下の囲み内の表現を使いながら英語で相談してみましょう。

> ***Useful phrases***　この表現を使って話し合ってみよう
>
> What did you hear for number ~ ?　　How do you spell ~ ?
> I heard ~　　　　　　　　　　　　　I think it's spelled _ _ _ _ _

　　　　　Words or expressions　　　Meaning in English or Japanese

1. _____ _____
2. _____ _____
3. _____ _____
4. _____ _____
5. _____ _____
6. _____ _____
7. _____ _____
8. _____ _____
9. _____ _____
10. _____ _____
11. _____ _____
12. _____ _____
13. _____ _____
14. _____ _____
15. _____ _____

3 Definitions

3、4人のグループを作ります。下の囲み内の表現を使って話し合いながら、2 で書き取ったそれぞれの語句の意味を簡潔な英語で説明してみましょう。英語での説明が難しい場合は、日本語の意味を記入しましょう。すべての単語について話し合ってから、答えを確認しましょう。

Useful phrases　この表現を使って話し合ってみよう

What does ~ mean in English?　　　　　　　I'm not sure. Maybe it is ~
I think so too.　　　　　　　　　OR　　　I agree.
I disagree. I think it means ~ .　　　OR　　　I think it's ~ in Japanese.

答えの確認が終わったグループは次の表現を使ってグループの成果を発表しなさい。

1. We knew the meanings of ____ words in Japanese.
2. We remembered the meaning of____ words in English.

SHORT DIALOG

下のそれぞれの文を読んでみましょう。ペアの相手と話し合って、それぞれが誰による発言だったかを思い出してみましょう。いくつ思い出せますか。その際、下の英語表現を使いながら英語で相談してみましょう。本書の登場人物一覧は次の頁にあります。

Useful Expressions

Who said ~?
Was it ~?　　　　　　　　　　　　OR　　　I think it was~
I can't remember. Let's look for the answer.

---

1. I'm from China. (   )
2. There will be a welcome party for you from 6:30 to 9:00 pm. in the cafeteria.
　　　　　　　　　　　　　　　　　　　　　　　　　(   )
3. I've heard a lot about you. (   )
4. Do you have any questions you'd like to ask me? (   )
5. Would you prefer a window or an aisle seat? (   )
6. What's your major, Jack? (   )
7. He is so helpful to all the exchange students. (   )
8. There is plenty to eat and drink so dig in! (   )
9. I'm looking forward to having dinner with you tonight. (   )
10. You should make a list of the things you want to pack. (   )

CHARACTER LIST:
Mr. Price, ticket agent, Sue Fisher, Sharon Smith, Jack, Jenny, Rosy, Toshi, Tony Jones, Candy (Chongdé)

PRONUNCIATION

1 Practice 1

下のそれぞれの語句をなめらかにつなげて発音したとき、どのような発音になるか覚えていますか。例にならってなめらかにつながった発音のつづりを記入しましょう。完成したら、ペアになって該当する頁で確認して通常の発音と音同士がつながった形の両方の発音を練習しましょう。

1. Sort of   (p.4)   Sorta
2. I would   (p.10) _____
3. Should have   (p.16) _____
4. Meet you   (p.22) _____
5. Did you   (p.28) _____
6. Going to   (p.34) _____
7. It will   (p.40) _____
8. Go over   (p.46) _____
9. Don't you   (p.64) _____
10. Like her   (p.76) _____

2 Practice 2 [CD 2–66~67/DL 155~156]

音声を聞いて、1～10の例文を完成させましょう。ここでは音同士がつながった形の文が流れますが、正しいつづりを書きます。完成させたらペア相手と交互に例文を発音してみましょう。

1. I feel _____ nervous.
2. What _____ say your name was?
3. You _____ asked for help.
4. Let's _____ there.
5. Why _____ get a job?
6. Are you _____ go to the festival?
7. I thought you'd _____.
8. It's nice to _____.
9. _____ be a lot of fun.
10. _____ like an aisle seat please.

SPEAKING   [Getting ready to go abroad]

1 Practice 1

あなたは今から一年間海外留学をすると想像してみましょう。出発前にするべきことや、購入しておくべきものは何でしょうか。

まず、下の欄に自分の必要項目（すること、買うもの）のリストを記入します。次に、ペアの相手と囲み内の表現を使いながらお互いのリストについて話し合ってみます。自分にあてはまるものがあれば、相手のリストから自分のリストに項目を加えていきましょう。

PREPARATION FOR STUDY ABROAD

Five things I need to do	Five things I need to buy

> **Useful Expressions**
>
> What should you *do / buy* before going abroad to study?
> Why do you want to _____ before you go abroad to study?
> Why do you need to buy a / an _____?
>
> I should _____ before I go abroad because _____.
> I need to buy a/an _____ because _____.

2 Practice 2

まず下の質問を読み、あなたの答えを英語で記入しなさい。次にペアになってお互いにこの質問をし合って相手の意見を聞きましょう。答える場合にはなるべく自分の書いたものは見ないで答えます。そのあとで、3〜4人のグループになってみんなで質問し合ってみましょう。同じような考えの人はいましたか。

Would you like to go abroad for a year like Toshi did? Why or why not?

_____
_____
_____

PROVERBS AND SAYINGS

まず、自分が好きな日本のことわざ（名言）を下の欄に記入してみましょう。次に3, 4人のグループになってお互いのことわざ（名言）の中から一つを選んで英語に訳してみましょう。最後に皆で協力しながら、そのことわざ（名言）の意味（真意）を英語で説明してみましょう。

Example:

A favorite proverb or saying:「早起きは三文の得」
In English: The early bird gets the worm.
Message: The person who arrives first or does things right away without waiting has the best chance of success.

My favorite proverb or saying (in Japanese):
_____

My group's proverb or saying (in Japanese):

_____

Translate it into English:

_____
_____
_____

What message does it communicate?

_____
_____
_____

音声ダウンロードについて

本書の音声は以下より無料でダウンロードできます。予習、復習にご利用ください。（2015年4月1日開始予定）

www.otowatsurumi.com/m3x7h3n9

上記 URL をブラウザのアドレスバーに直接入力して下さい。パソコンでのご利用をお勧めします。圧縮ファイル (zip) ですのでスマートフォンでの場合は事前に解凍アプリをご用意下さい。

◉本書別売 CD をご希望の方はお近くの書店にご注文下さい。
（定価：本体 2,000 円＋税）

Sounds Real!
Authentic Listening and Speaking Practice

おもいっきり英語コミュニケーション

編著者	Allyson MacKenzie
	安 山 秀 盛
発行者	山 口 隆 史

発 行 所　　株式会社 音羽書房鶴見書店

〒113-0033　東京都文京区本郷4-1-14
TEL 03-3814-0491
FAX 03-3814-9250
URL: http://www.otowatsurumi.com
e-mail: info@otowatsurumi.com

2015年3月1日　　初版発行
2017年4月1日　　3刷発行

組版　ほんのしろ
装幀　熊谷有紗（オセロ）
印刷・製本　(株)シナノ
■ 落丁・乱丁本はお取り替えいたします。

EC-062